The Hal
Comedy ⌐⌐⌐⌐
of Thelma Todd, ZaSu Pitts
and Patsy Kelly

ALSO BY JAMES L. NEIBAUR
AND FROM MCFARLAND

The Films of Jean Harlow (2019)

The Andy Clyde Columbia Comedies (2018)

The W.C. Fields Films (2017)

Chaplin at Essanay: A Film Artist in Transition, 1915–1916 (2008)

Arbuckle and Keaton: Their 14 Film Collaborations (2007)

*The RKO Features: A Complete Filmography
of the Feature Films Released or Produced
by RKO Radio Pictures, 1929–1960* (1994; paperback 2005)

The Bob Hope Films (2005)

BY JAMES L. NEIBAUR AND TED OKUDA

*The Jerry Lewis Films: An Analytical Filmography
of the Innovative Comic* (McFarland, 1994; paperback 2013)

The Hal Roach Comedy Shorts of Thelma Todd, ZaSu Pitts and Patsy Kelly

JAMES L. NEIBAUR

McFarland & Company, Inc., Publishers
Jefferson, North Carolina

ISBN (print) 978-1-4766-7255-7
ISBN (ebook) 978-1-4766-3431-9

LIBRARY OF CONGRESS CATALOGUING-IN-PUBLICATION DATA

BRITISH LIBRARY CATALOGUING DATA ARE AVAILABLE

Front cover images: *top* ZaSu Pitts, Charles Gemora and Thelma Todd
in *Sealskins*; *bottom* Patsy Kelly and Thelma Todd in *Babes in the Goods*

Printed in the United States of America

*McFarland & Company, Inc., Publishers
Box 611, Jefferson, North Carolina 28640
www.mcfarlandpub.com*

To Dave Lord Heath.
Thanks for adding so much to this project
with your tireless research
and never "falling down" on the job.

Acknowledgments

Special thanks go to Katie Carter, who lives every book with me, watching the films, adding her own observations, and catching my typos. I don't know what I did without her—but then I realize my first two books were written before she was born!

Very special thanks to Dave Lord Heath, whose website on the Hal Roach productions is filled with factual information from his painstaking research. Dave was always there whenever I needed the tiniest bit of information, and his help on this project was invaluable.

Thanks to Richard Finegan for providing many wonderful photo illustrations, and to Greg Hilbrich for helping me round up all the movies.

Michelle Morgan, who wrote the definitive biography of Thelma Todd, was kind, supportive and encouraging. I appreciated her help when I need to verify a fact.

Thanks to my late friend Charles Stumpf who wrote the definitive biography of ZaSu Pitts, which was released the year after his 2009 passing.

Special thanks to the late Patsy Kelly and George "Spanky" McFarland for taking the time to talk to a fan many years ago.

Thanks also to Ted Okuda, Benny Drinnon, Richard Bann, Leonard Maltin, Max Neibaur, Kelly Parmelee, Allie Schulz, Terri Lynch, the late Jules White, Eve Golden, the late Jerry Lewis, Ron Hutchinson, George Willeman, Paul Gierucki, Craig Calman, Steve Massa, Irv Hyatt, Rob Stone, Nick Digilio, Dale Wamboldt, Dan Savino, Sim Gershon, Kit Parker, Alexandria Kaprelian, Lea Stans, Kim Morgan, Allan Ellenberger, the late David Shepard and Blackhawk Films.

Table of Contents

Introduction

When director Paul Feig's film *Bridemaids* was released in 2011, some critics celebrated the comedy by stating that it proved women could be funny. Had those critics any understanding of cinema's rich history, they would realize that this fact had been proven way back during the silent era, with such funny ladies as Mabel Normand, Alice Howell, Gale Henry, Dorothy Devore and many others.

Certainly one of the most naturally funny women in screen comedy was Thelma Todd. She originally aspired to be a dramatic actress, but her formidable flair for comedy led her to appearing in films with Buster Keaton, Laurel and Hardy, the Marx Brothers, Harry Langdon, Charley Chase, Wheeler and Woolsey and, beginning in 1931, her own series of short comedies for the Hal Roach Studios. First Thelma was teamed with ZaSu Pitts. After Pitts left the studio in 1933, Thelma was teamed with Patsy Kelly. When Thelma died tragically in 1935, Patsy tried to carry on, first with Pert Kelton, then with Lyda Roberti, but the series ended in 1937 when Roberti left movies due to poor health (she died the following year).

While these teams have been acknowledged in a few sources (most notably Leonard Maltin's books *The Great Movie Shorts* and *Movie Comedy Teams*), this is the first book-length study specifically discussing the comedies. I will go film by film, in chronological order, and for each movie I will provide credits, plot information, an analysis noting any common themes, and offer as much background information as my research could uncover. Because these two-reel comedies have never enjoyed individual in-depth coverage, a good amount of the information contained here will be exclusive to this book, as will be many of our photo illustrations and graphics. An added bit of significance includes memories from one of the stars. When Patsy Kelly appeared in a play near where I was living in the 1970s, she was kind enough to accept a phone call at the theater and answer some questions. I was calling her as a fan, not as an interviewer, so her quotes from this makeshift interview are seeing print for the first time in this book.

Although there will be biographical details offered along the way when they are pertinent to our study, this book does not pretend to be a biography. There are biographies of Thelma Todd that investigate her personal life, including her romances, her marriage, her connection with unsavory characters, and various theories regarding her untimely death. While this text will certainly acknowledge what's out there, we make no attempt to understand, or to solve an unsolved crime from over 80 years ago. Any reference to such events in Todd's life will be as it pertains to her work.

Ad slick used in newspapers to promote a Todd–Kelly comedy.

This book focuses specifically on the series of two-reelers that Thelma–ZaSu–Patsy made for Hal Roach. However, each actress was very active outside of the series. The Hal Roach Studio took time off each year, allowing its actors to pursue opportunities elsewhere. Many of this performers did not work outside of their own series, but Todd, Pitts and Kelly all did.. These other appearances will be mentioned as we go, when significant to the performer's overall career.

The comedies in this series are creative and funny, and set the foundation for a lot of later examples (e.g. the Lucille Ball–Vivian Vance teaming on TV). Each individual short has its own level of significance. The series evolved creatively and responded to several different directors, some of whom worked well with this concept, some who did not. When Gus Meins was signed to direct the shorts, a consistent style was honed. The formula was already beginning to take hold, but when Meins was consistently working on the films, it became more effective. Meins left the series when Roach decided he should exclusively direct the Our Gang series, but he occasionally returned. Thelma,

ZaSu and Patsy also responded well to directors George Marshall, James Parrott and William Terhune.

This text will specifically address these various aspects of the films, including the influence of the director. I will discuss the films that more closely examine the on-screen relationship, those that spotlight one performer over the other, ideas that work and those that don't. Overall, this book is an appreciation of a very amusing, creative series that most certainly offers a lot of examples as to how funny women could be many decades before the release of *Bridesmaids*.

1

The Early Life
of Thelma Todd

Thelma Alice Todd was born in Lawrence, Massachusetts, on July 29, 1906. Her initial aspiration to become a schoolteacher was disrupted by her entering beauty contests, resulting in her winning the title of Miss Massachusetts in 1925. Spotted by a Hollywood talent agent, Thelma was invited to move to New York and enroll in a new Paramount School, created by the studio's president Jesse Lasky, to cultivate new film actors and actresses. Much to the chagrin of her father, Thelma accepted, believing that if she was dissatisfied she could always take the next train home.

At the Paramount School, Thelma had trouble taking things seriously. She frequently joked around, causing a reaction of consternation from her teachers and distracting many of the other students. Eventually she connected with some of the people in the school, engaged more in the activities, and was cast, along with many other students, in the Sam Wood film *Fascinating Youth* (1926). While this was an exciting time for Thelma, she was shattered when, on her 20th birthday in July 1926, her father died suddenly of a heart attack.

Despite this tragedy, Thelma soldiered on, appearing in a small role in the movie *God Gave Me Twenty Cents* (1926) and securing the leading lady role in the Ed Wynn comedy *Rubber Heels* (1927). Shortly thereafter, the studio sent her to work in Hollywood. Thelma was delighted. In her first Hollywood film she appeared with Gary Cooper and William Powell in *Nevada* (1927), followed by smaller roles in a few more films, before being cast as Richard Dix's leading lady in *The Gay Defender* (1927).

Thelma's career was jeopardized when she was invited to what turned out to be a wild Hollywood party where a studio executive propositioned her, and was annoyed that she chose to instead leave the party. She was threatened with being blacklisted and was fired from another proposed movie with Dix, *Sporting Goods* (1928), and replaced by Gertrude Olmstead. Shortly thereafter, First National bought her contract from Jesse Lasky.

At First National, Todd realized she had a real flair for playing comedy when cast with Charlie Murray and Louise Fazenda in *Vamping Venus* (1928). She appeared in several films for First National, and as silent movies gave way to talkies, she made the transition successfully. But by the end of the 1920s, she was freelancing, no longer under contract to any studio.

While still interested in pursuing a career as a dramatic actress, Thelma's natural flair for comedy led her to the Hal Roach Studios, where she appeared in the very first sound movie featuring the popular screen duo Stan Laurel and Oliver Hardy, then at the height of their career. Laurel and Hardy had teamed a couple of years earlier, and by 1929 they were already being hailed as comic geniuses. That year is considered perhaps their richest year in films, including such silent classics as *Big Business* and two films featuring future MGM star Jean Harlow, *Dou-*

Thelma Todd in 1927.

ble Whoopee and *Bacon Grabbers*. The duo's talkie debut *Unaccustomed As We Are* included, along with Thelma, Edgar Kennedy and Mae Busch, veteran comedians whose career dated back to Mack Sennett's Keystone period. Thelma not only held her own, she managed to stand out among these top comic stars.

In 1930, Howard Hughes released his epic feature *Hell's Angels* which he'd begun a couple years earlier as a silent and reshot as a sound film. It made Harlow a star. Thelma had appeared in some scenes but by the time *Hell's Angels* was released, her footage had been jettisoned.

Thelma remained active in comedies for Roach, including Harry Langdon's sound debut with the studio, *Hotter Than Hot* (1929), as well as other Langdon sound comedies such as *The Head Guy*, *The Fighting Parson*, *The Shrimp* and *The King* (all 1930). Thelma also appeared in several Charley Chase movies including *Snappy Sneezer*, *Crazy Feet* (1929), *The Real McCoy*, *Whispering Whoopee*, *All Teed Up*, *Dollar Dizzy*, *Looser Than Loose*, *High Seas*

Thelma poses with a group of puppies.

(1930) and *The Pip from Pittsburg* and *Rough Seas* (1931). She did some of her best work with Chase, and more of her great comedic work in the Laurel and Hardy comedies *Another Fine Mess* (1930) and *Chickens Come Home* (1931). Chase asked Roach if the two of them could be a permanent screen team, but the producer had other plans.

2

The Early Life
of ZaSu Pitts

Eliza Susan Pitts was born January 3, 1894, in Parsons, Kansas; her family moved to Santa Cruz, California, when she was nine. Her nickname "ZaSu" was taken from the last syllable of her first name and the first syllable of her middle name. Pronounced variously by whomever one asks, ZaSu herself indicated during her life that the correct pronunciation is "Say-soo" and that is how Thelma Todd addresses her in all of their films together.

A very bashful child, ZaSu was encouraged by friends to join their school's theater department to help overcome her shyness. She was reticent at first, but soon realized that her natural stammering and nervous hand gestures lent themselves well to comic roles, while her forlorn facial expression was effective in drama. She overcame any inhibitions and grew into theater acting. ZaSu enjoyed success in several community theater productions before deciding to try finding work in the movie industry, traveling to Los Angeles at age 21. She managed to find extra work and small roles, her striking appearance and offbeat mannerisms once again causing her to stand out. Among those who took notice were screenwriter Frances Marion and director King Vidor, each of whom helped advance her career.

Pitts continued to use her natural appearance and mannerisms for both drama and comedy. Along with serious roles in films like the Frances Marion–penned *Little Princess* (1917), directed by Marshal Neilan, and King Vidor's *Better Times* (1919), she also co-starred in a series of one-reel comedies for Universal, replacing the recently departed Gale Henry opposite comedian Billy Franey. In 1920 she married Tom Gallery, an actor with whom she'd worked in several films.

In 1924 alone, Pitts appeared in ten movies. Over this time she settled more comfortably into comic roles, but that did not stop Erich von Stroheim from casting her in his 1924 epic *Greed*, for which Pitts won great acclaim. The filmmaker proclaimed her to be the greatest dramatic actress in movies,

ZaSu Pitts in 1925.

despite her flair for comedy. Von Stroheim used her again in other films such as *The Wedding March* (1928).

Comfortably making the transition to sound films, Pitts had settled almost exclusively into the comedy genre when she was cast as the mother of Lew Ayers in Lewis Milestone's *All Quiet on the Western Front* (1930). However, this serious dramatic role drew laughs from the audience who had gotten used to Pitts playing humorous roles. Milestone begrudgingly replaced her scenes with new footage of Beryl Mercer playing the mother. This event was a big disappointment for ZaSu, who took her craft quite seriously and could not understand why she was not accepted by audiences as an actress who did both dramatic and comedic roles.

As had happened for Thelma Todd, ZaSu's natural flair for comedy led her to Hal Roach Studios where in 1931 Roach got the idea to create a female pair of slapstick comedians as a counterpart to his successful Laurel and Hardy films. Roach thought that Pitts and his other top comic Todd would be a female version of Laurel and Hardy, but not exactly with the same dynamic.

Hal Roach had enjoyed real success by doing a lot of experimenting with different ideas. His plan to create a series of comedies featuring children in simple comic situations begat the Our Gang series, which had enjoyed popularity since the silent era and with an evolving series of actors as the youngsters outgrew their parts. Laurel and Hardy had certainly made an impact, as had Charley Chase.

Roach believed that Thelma's established style and character would play off of ZaSu's effectively. Pitts and Todd both agreed to the teaming, but with

"GIRLS! YOU MADE GOOD!"

HAL ROACH presents
8 COMEDIES *starring*
ZASU PITTS
THELMA TODD

Hal Roach promoted Thelma and ZaSu's films heavily in the trades.

the understanding that they would be allowed to take other roles outside of the studio and not be limited to a two-reel comedy series. Each had aspirations for roles other than comedy, and ZaSu especially did not want to find herself typecast in slapstick. The disappointment of the *All Quiet on the Western Front* situation was still recent. Hal Roach agreed to these terms, and the two actresses started work on their first project. It helped that they hit if off as friends almost immediately, making the set a very cohesive working environment. This was an off-screen friendship that helped bolster the realistic quality of their on-screen relationship. Their first film together was a three-reel comedy entitled *Let's Do Things*, directed by Hal Roach himself.

3

The Films of Thelma Todd and ZaSu Pitts

Let's Do Things (1931)

Produced and Directed by Hal Roach; *Dialogue by* H.M. Walker; *Cinematographer:* George Stevens; *Editor:* Richard Currier; *Cast:* Thelma Todd, ZaSu Pitts, George Byron, Jerry Mandy, Harry Bernard, Charlie Hall, Maurice Black, Baldwin Cooke, Venice Lloyd, Mickey Daniels, Edward Dillon, Ham Kinsey, Gordon Douglas, Bill Elliott, Dorothy Granger, Mary Kornman, Gertrude Messinger, Donald Novis, Charley Rogers, David Sharpe, LeRoy Shield, Clara Guiol, William Gillespie; *Released by* MGM on June 6, 1931; Three Reels

When Hal Roach got the idea to put Thelma Todd and ZaSu Pitts together, his idea for a female Laurel and Hardy wasn't an immediate concept. He just felt, at the outset, that the attractive, sarcastic comic persona Todd had established would play well off of the fluttery character for which Pitts had become known in comedy.

At this time, Roach was experimenting with the three-reel format (most of his short comedies ran two reels). Roach felt that a longer subject could perhaps take the place of a second feature and generate greater revenue for the studio. This worked sometimes, when a film like Laurel and Hardy's three-reel *The Music Box* (1932) ended up with an Oscar for Best Short Subject (live action). But sometimes the three-reelers seemed a bit protracted, and such is the case with *Let's Do Things*.

Perhaps it would have been better if the first teaming of Todd and Pitts featured them in a more compact two-reeler. While *Let's Do Things* has some funny moments, and does a good job of establishing the duo's chemistry, it would likely have worked better at a shorter length without, for instance, a distracting acrobatic musical number during a nightclub scene.

This film features the girls as roommates who also work together at a

11

Left to right: Jerry Mandy, George Byron, ZaSu Pitts and Thelma Todd in *Let's Do Things* **(1931).**

large department store, plugging songs and selling sheet music. Thelma doesn't like ZaSu's freeloading boyfriend Milton (George Byron) but when he asks them out for the evening, along with a doctor friend (Jerry Mandy), they accept, but only after Milton tells them that the doctor is paying for everything. The doctor appears to be a boorish quack, and Thelma has misgivings about going out, but the four of them end up at a club. While watching the floor show, the doctor produces a bottle of homemade liquor (this movie was made during Prohibition) and most of it ends up in ZaSu's ginger ale. Thelma wants to get rid of the men, so she pretends to be drunk and disruptive. When ZaSu acts the same way from actually being drunk, Thelma commends her "act." During a wild dance number, the doctor ends up flying off of the dance floor onto a table, face first in a bowl of spaghetti, and gets tossed out by an angry waiter (Charlie Hall). ZaSu, Thelma and Milton end up back at the girls' apartment. When he asks for a piece of pie, Thelma tosses it in his face, ending the short. Within this plot structure there are several funny gags and situations, and each woman is given the opportunity to exhibit her own comic talent and the effectiveness of the team dynamic.

The film opens with Thelma in the store, at the piano playing and singing the Maceo Pinkard–Doris Tauber–William Tracey composition "Them There Eyes," published in 1930. (It became a very popular song and eventually a standard.) She is joined by a sextet of men harmonizing, but they are stopped by the boss (Ed Dillon), who orders everyone back to work. This scene immediately introduces Thelma as the pretty, talented one who is in control of the situation, and fluttery ZaSu as the off-key croaker who needs to keep quiet and make the sales. ZaSu's stammering delivery of her lines in that first scene establish her as being much meeker and more hesitant than Thelma. And the lines themselves, as she's trying to sell sheet music, are funny too: "'I'm Throwing Myself Away,' for only 25 cents!"

Todd's establishing scene in this short was derived from her own real-life experience. According to Roach studio publicity, Thelma's first job was selling sheet music at a music store, and she evidently attracted a lot of male attention. Of course this could merely be studio puffery, but it is interesting that publicity Roach used to promote Todd found its way into her first comedy with Pitts.

Despite her aversion to Milton, the prospect of a doctor from Boston sounds good to Thelma, but these hopes are dashed upon his first appearance and she feigns a headache. Jerry Mandy plays the doctor in a delightfully boisterous manner, insisting his gimmicky cures for the spine are foolproof. Almost immediately he demonstrates on a skeptical Thelma by wrestling her around as she sits on her bed, insisting he can cure her headache. This bit of slapstick roughhousing establishes the fact that these ladies planned to engage in the same kind of physical comedy as any men on the lot. The doctor states, "I'll stay until you're normal if it takes all night." That is what inspires Thelma to go out, stating, "I don't want to get my neck broke." George Byron and Jerry Mandy's style of humor complements Thelma and ZaSu nicely without overwhelming or taking the spotlight from them. We also see the difference in ZaSu and Thelma's personalities in their interactions with them, especially with Milton. ZaSu is very hesitant around him and almost seems eager to please, while Thelma is rather bossy.

Much of the humor is situational and there are many set-ups that lead to other amusing situations. ZaSu doesn't have shoes that look good in formal attire, so she uncomfortably squeezes into a pair of Thelma's. When they show up at the club and ZaSu's coat is removed, she is visibly wearing an undershirt beneath her gown. In a funny bit, Thelma quickly decides to drag

ZaSu into the ladies room and fix things, but accidentally grabs the arm of a drunk (Charley Rogers) who is then tossed out by an angry maid.

Once the couples are at their table, the doctor tries to play footsie with Thelma. She kicks at him and ends up kicking away ZaSu's shoes, which she has taken off to rest her aching feet. This leads to a couple of funny situations, the first of which has a shoeless ZaSu dancing with Milton, getting gum on the bottom of her stockinged foot. Later, ZaSu crawls around under tables looking for her shoes, getting her hand stepped on by patrons.

The doctor's inability as a chiropractor leads to a particularly amusing floor show situation. When the lead dancer of a chorus (Dorothy Granger)

Left to right: Thelma Todd, Charley Rogers, ZaSu Pitts and Mickey Daniels in *Let's Do Things* (1931).

falls down injured, the doctor goes backstage to assist her. When he returns to the table, he states that he fixed up the spines of all the dancers. The film then cuts to the chorus coming out on stage, hunched over in pain and unable to perform their routine.

It would be interesting to know how much cinematographer George Stevens contributed to this short. Stevens went on to become one of the top directors of American cinema, helming such features as *Gunga Din* (1939), *Shane* (1953) and *Giant* (1956). There is some impressive camerawork in *Let's Do Things*, including the establishing shots in the department store and the nightclub (the latter shot from a lower level, through a table where patrons are sitting). The close-ups of Jerry Mandy and Todd, the former trying to play footsie with the latter, show their facial expressions, adding more humor to the scene. The cuts to Thelma's double-take reactions punctuate a lot of the gags. There are also quick visual bits like ZaSu absent-mindedly putting a megaphone in ink and then making an imprint on her face when she uses it, and Thelma yelping when she sits on the hard bristles of an upturned hair brush.

A year earlier, Hal Roach began a comedy shorts series called The Boy Friends featuring teenagers (actually young adults) after the success of his Our Gang comedies featuring children. Todd appeared in the Boy Friends short Love Fever earlier this same year, playing an actress rehearsing a murder scene in her apartment. The kids think they are hearing the real thing, which results in several comical misunderstandings. Several Boy Friends performers appear in this movie. Mickey Daniels offers his cackling hyena laugh as the busboy who removes ZaSu's coat at the club. David Sharpe and Gertrude Messinger are acrobatic dancers in one of the musical numbers. Mary Kornman is a gum-chewing cigarette girl.

In the September 5, 1931, issue of *Motion Picture World*, columnist J.C. Jenkins stated, "*Let's Do Things* is a bang-up good comedy with ZaSu Pitts and Thelma Todd doing the most of the funny stuff."[1] In the February 1932 *New Movie Magazine*, moviegoer Juanita Loper wrote, "*Let's Do Things* gave me the biggest laugh of the season. Thelma Todd and ZaSu Pitts make a very clever team and I know film fans would enjoy seeing them together again. More joy and laughter, and less thought of the Depression."[2]

Let's Do Things was an effective debut for the team of Todd and Pitts, and Roach immediately began planning more films with them together. However, this movie was shot just before the studio's annual six-week sabbatical when no production took place. This gave Hal Roach a chance to test the waters regarding his new female comedy team. *Let's Do Things* was successful enough to continue to team Todd and Pitts.

During this time, Thelma went over to Warner Brothers and appeared opposite Joe E. Brown in *Broadminded* (1931) while ZaSu had a role in the RKO feature *A Woman of Experience* and the Fox film *Their Mad Moment*. She was billed third in each. Upon completing these projects, the women were back at the Roach studios in May 1931 to film their second short together.

Catch-As Catch-Can (1931)

Directed by Marshall Neilan; *Produced by* Hal Roach; *Dialogue by* H.M. Walker; *Cinematographer:* Art Lloyd; *Editor:* Richard Currier; *Cast:* Thelma Todd, ZaSu Pitts, Guinn "Big Boy" Williams, Reed Howes, Frank Alexander, Sammy Brooks, Al Cooke, Edward Dillon, Billy Gilbert, Buster Brodie, Bud Duncan, Estelle Etterre, Ivan Linow, Ham Kinsey, Gordon Douglas, Dick Gilbert, Kit Guard; *Released by* MGM on August 22, 1931; Two Reels

When the success of *Let's Do Things* satisfied Hal Roach enough to continue teaming Todd and Pitts, the studio's gag men got to work creating situations that would work with their distinctive characters. *Catch-As Catch-Can* maintained the same relationship between the two as in the previous film, with Thelma the wisecracking leader and ZaSu the fluttery follower. This time the girls are switchboard operators. Thelma is dating a wrestling manager, while ZaSu falls for the wrestler.

It opens with Thelma and ZaSu conversing in a manner that may not have been carefully scripted. It appears to be simply a conversation between the two as they get ready to begin work at the switchboard. ZaSu is in a nearby fashion store trying on expensive hats when Thelma summons her to the switchboard. They start conversing casually about how they need the job, with ZaSu indicating she'd rather be back home on the farm milking contented cows. It all has a very natural feel, as if improvised, and if it is indeed scripted, the performances are quite brilliant. There is some absurd comedy with a drunk (Al Cooke) who hands the girls the phone from his room, indicating that it is out of order, so he is directed to a phone booth in the lobby. A previous caller had flowers, and a bee from the bouquet has settled into the phone's earpiece. The buzzing confuses the drunk into believing he keeps getting a busy signal.

The connection between ZaSu and wrestler Strangler Sullivan (Guinn

"Big Boy" Williams) is that he is also homesick for a simpler life. Thelma's beau is Strangler's manager Harry (Reed Howes), who must control his destructive protégé by keeping his frustrations from manifesting themselves physically (tearing off doors, lifting a heavy trunk and crashing it through the floor). The fact that this is a pre–Code film is indicated by a scene where Harry hires several attractive women to "keep Strangler company and his mind off of being homesick." He finds his way to the lobby and that is when he and ZaSu connect. It is an amusing connection in that they bond over their homesickness and longing to be back on the farm (Strangler says he is from Lawrence, Kansas—ZaSu was actually from the state of Kansas, while Thelma was actually from the town of Lawrence, but in Massachusetts). Strangler asks Thelma how to get in good with ZaSu, and she suggests he buy her the expensive hat that attracted her in the boutique. He does so, and leaves ZaSu a note saying that if she loves him she should wear the hat to his wrestling bout that night. The next scene shows the girls headed to their seats in a crowded arena, with ZaSu wearing that elaborate hat.

All of this is merely the set-up for the arena scenes which take up the body of the film, as the girls attend a wrestling bout where several outrageous slapstick incidents occur. Director Marshall Neilan's filling the negative space in the frame with tightly packed spectators gives a nice claustrophobic image, with cutaways to an outrageous wrestling bout that is the preliminary before Strangler fights. There are a lot of clever and amusing ideas used during this sequence. The wrestlers lock up and move about the ring while the crowd sarcastically sings "Let Me Call You Sweetheart" as if they are locked in a romantic embrace on a dance floor. Once the grapplers are in the clinches on the mat, the smaller wrestler starts tickling the larger one, and as his opponent laughs he complains, "You promised me you wouldn't!" At another point during this preliminary bout, a wrestler's head is banged onto the mat repeatedly so an enterprising ringside spectator puts walnuts down and gets them cracked open.

Rather than jump to the wrestling match in which Strangler is to appear, the choice is made to have an opening bout during which Thelma and ZaSu can establish their place in the audience. Cutting away to comic sequences going on in the ring adds a bit more substance to the scene.

When Strangler gets in the ring to battle against Stromboni (played by wrestler turned actor Ivan Linow). ZaSu's wide-brimmed hat is causing a problem, and this results in a bit of a tussle with nearby spectators. One of them removes her hat and throws it. She chases after it and another spectator

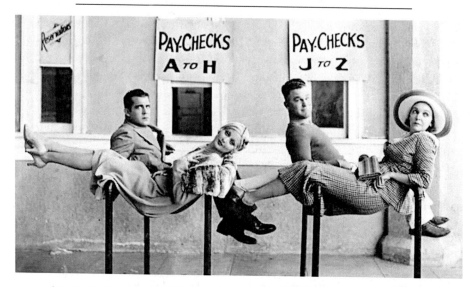

Left to right: Reed Howes, Thelma Todd, Guinn "Big Boy" Williams and ZaSu Pitts in *Catch-As Catch-Can* (1931).

tosses it in the other direction. A beaten and battered ZaSu returns to her seat, her hat tied to her head, and yells to get Strangler's attention. When he sees her in the audience, he excitedly becomes more aggressive with his opponent and tosses him out of the ring, winning the bout. When his hand is raised, Thelma and ZaSu run to the ring to congratulate him. A mouse crawls into the ring, causing Strangler to scream and faint as the film concludes.

The two-reel *Catch-As Catch-Can* is sillier and funnier than the duo's three-reel debut as a team. Guinn "Big Boy" Williams had established himself in the silent era, playing brutish characters and amiable oafs, and he continued to do so well into the television era. An actual rancher's son, Williams was often cast in westerns. He only appeared in a few Roach films. In an interview, Williams stated, "I worked all the time, 12 pictures a year, but I hated every one of them. I never studied a script. I'd glance over my part just before a scene and bluff it through. I lived to drink and play polo."[3] Williams' good friend, actor Will Rogers, gave Williams his "Big Boy" nickname and introduced him to the game of polo. He was known as the Babe Ruth of the elite sport.

As the wrestler's manager, Reed Howes is appearing in his one and only Roach film out of nearly 300 acting appearances in films and TV. During the silent era, Howes had been a leading man.

Marshall Neilan was a top director during the silent era, working for Goldwyn and Louis B. Mayer before the two formed MGM. Neilan's dislike for Mayer resulted in his refusing to continue with the studio after the merge. By the time talkies arrived, Neilan was plagued by a serious drinking problem. Hal Roach, whose films were released through MGM, was among the few producers who would hire him. He does an excellent job with the crowd scenes and slapstick pandemonium in the audience during *Catch-As Catch-Can*'s wrestling sequences. Once Strangler sees ZaSu wearing the hat and begins to fight more aggressively in the ring, the action is sped up. The film's two reel length was wrapping up by that time, so this might have been more of a cost-saving measure rather than an aesthetic choice. Neilan would direct Todd and Pitts again.

In a *Film Daily* review, the critic called this "a good comedy [with] plenty of action and enough laughs to satisfy."[4] It was an improvement over their first short, being more streamlined and featuring more consistent gag sequences. The characters continue to be appealing and the structure of having a set-up followed by more raucous slapstick worked effectively.

After completing filming of this short, Thelma had a strong supporting role in the Marx Brothers feature *Monkey Business* at Paramount. As the character Lucille, she has many scenes with Groucho Marx, trading lines with him as straight woman in the same manner as she performed with ZaSu Pitts—of course with the understanding that Groucho was a much different comedian. She connected well with his absurdity:

GROUCHO: Madam, before I get through with you, you will have a clear case for divorce, and so will my wife. Now, the first thing to do is to arrange for a settlement. You take the children, your husband takes the house, Junior burns down the house, you take the insurance, and I take you.
LUCILLE: But I haven't any children.
GROUCHO: That's just the trouble with this country. You haven't any children, and as for me, I'm going back in the closet where men are empty overcoats.
LUCILLE: Oh, brown eyes…

At one point in *Monkey Business*, Groucho tells Thelma, "You're a woman who's been getting nothing but dirty breaks. Well, we can clean and tighten your brakes, but you'll have to stay in the garage all night." This is a rather chilling line when one remembers how Todd's life ended four years later. *Monkey Business* was Thelma's first time in a Marx Brothers film, but not her last.

The Pajama Party (1931)

Produced and Directed by Hal Roach; *Titles by* H.M. Walker; *Cinematographer:* Walter Lundin; *Editor:* Richard Currier; *Cast:* Thelma Todd, ZaSu Pitts, Elizabeth Forrester, Eddie Dunn, Donald Novis, Lucien Prival, Billy Gilbert, Charlie Hall, Sydney Jarvis, Frank Terry, Germaine De Neel, John J. Richardson; *Released by* MGM on October 3, 1931; Two Reels

The Pajama Party shows Thelma and ZaSu still exploring their on-screen relationship while continuing to play characters they'd already established as solo actresses. For the most part, it is effective, as their separate personalities blend nicely.

It appears by this, the duo's third short together, that the structure of Thelma and ZaSu humorously responding to their situation is the formula being utilized for the series. Thelma is again the smart, resourceful one, while ZaSu is fluttery and forlorn.

This time the girls work at a broadcasting company where their boyfriends (Eddie Dunn and Donald Novis) sing in a band. The band is hired to play at a posh all-night party, so plans are made for Thelma and ZaSu to drive ahead and spend a quiet evening, and then the next morning they can all go for a swim. En route, the girls are run off the road and their car plunges into a lake. The woman who caused the accident, a wealthy society lady, invites them to her luxurious mansion to dry off. She is giving a party for a Baron Mittenhuasen (Lucien Prival), and the girls are invited to attend. The behavior of the society people is anything but staid, as they take turns kicking the backside of a man celebrating his birthday, and cavort and sing in a silly manner. Thelma and ZaSu start having fun with the kooky goings-on, and the men are all quite attracted to Miss Todd. This opening scene with the girls and the band also helps to set up their characters for the film, as all the men surround Thelma, singing to her, while ZaSu remains aloof. This dynamic would be revisited later in the film.

The lady of the house asks servants to take care of the girls, including allowing them a bath and a change of clothes. ZaSu is appalled when the French maid, who doesn't speak English, tries to undress her for a bath. Thelma, responding much better to her surroundings and enjoying the pampering (she responds to her French maid with pig Latin), ends up stumbling fully clothed into a full bathtub. In another funny bit, ZaSu's maid laughs uproariously at her underwear, until ZaSu lifts the maid's skirt and reveals her undergarments are the same design.

20

When plain, sad-faced ZaSu is introduced around, there is little reaction. As soon as Thelma joins the party, the men immediately flock around her (a fun visual has short Charlie Hall struggling to find an opening in the crowd of men surrounding Thelma, so he can move in nearer). Hal Roach's direction never has the distinct vision of other directors at his studio, but his choice to cut to a close-up of Thelma as she enters the party, and then cut away to the close-up expressions of several of the men, has a nice rhythm and makes a good comic effect.

As a running gag, ZaSu sees a lineup of partygoers kicking another as a customary birthday activity. Having been told by Thelma to fit in by observing and copying, ZaSu takes to kicking anyone who bends over, including the butler and the visiting baron. When she kicks the drunken Charlie Hall, he kicks her backside in return.

The conflict is presented when Thelma walks out to the pool area surrounded by men and her boyfriend in the band has a jealous reaction. Thelma is propositioned by a series of men, who ask her if she wants to "see the Japanese pagoda." She goes off with each one, in an effort to make her boyfriend jealous. Each time they wander off, and shortly thereafter come back with the man sporting a black eye. This shows a comic version of an empowered woman on a couple of levels: Thelma takes control of a situation in which she is innocent and her boyfriend stubbornly refuses to listen, and she also isn't about to be taken advantage of by these privileged rich men. Partly because of scenes like this, these humorous films still hold up well in the 21st century.

ZaSu's jealous boyfriend gets even by sticking a small live turtle from a fishbowl down her back. As the turtle maneuvers about, ZaSu reacts in a herky-jerky manner, and then slaps nearby Charlie Hall, believing he pinched her. Meanwhile, the baron remains upset over ZaSu having kicked him earlier, so he complains to the hostess and she explains why the girls are at the party. Their boyfriends overhear, and all is forgiven. But ZaSu still has the turtle down her back, and a good pinch causes her to make wild, spastic gestures that result in her involuntarily pushing several patrons into the pool. Just as the boyfriends walk up and indicate they now realize what happened, the hostess asks them all to leave. As the hostess bends over to help the other guests out of the pool, ZaSu gives one last kick for good measure.

Variety called this knockabout comedy an "old fashioned two-reeler idea but with the sex angle reversed. Two women do the comedy and take the falls. They're Thelma Todd and ZaSu Pitts, a first-rate team with all the

Thelma Todd is caught in a tub in *The Pajama Party* (1931).

requirements. Together they make this short interesting. Todd and Pitts could continue indefinitely as a combination for the two-reelers. They make the old gags appear slightly different."[5] *Film Daily* was less impressed and dismissed *The Pajama Party* as being only fair:

> This newly formed team will show to better advantage with stories that are stronger than this. However, there are many laughs due to Miss Pitts' unique style and droll delivery. There is much tomfoolery and slapstick stuff which results in a moderate number of laughs, the biggest coming when ZaSu tries to understand a French maid who insists on undressing her.[6]

The trades announced the filming of *The Pajama Party* and even indicated that Hal Roach planned to direct the film himself. Elizabeth Forrester, third-billed as the party hostess, is better known for her appearances in Roach comedies with Charley Chase or Todd and Pitts than her small parts in Paul Stein's *Born to Love* (1931) and Josef von Sternberg's *An American Tragedy* (1931). *The Pajama Party* is Forrester's second-to-last film (her last was *What a Bozo* [1931] with Charley Chase). In 2004, she died at age 96. Roach stalwart Charlie Hall has a funny series of bits as the drunken party guest. As a butler, the talented Billy Gilbert isn't given much to do. He would fare better in subsequent Todd–Pitts comedies.

As Thelma and ZaSu continued to hit their stride, the formidable Roach gag men continued to find situations and create gags that helped to enhance and spotlight their particular talents. After filming *The Pajama Party*, the busy ZaSu appeared in the First National feature *Penrod and Sam* for William Beaudine (who specifically requested her services), and also co-starred with the celebrated Alfred Lunt and Lynn Fontanne in MGM's *The Guardsman*.

War Mamas (1931)

Directed by Marshall Neilan; *Dialogue by* H.M. Walker; *Produced by* Hal Roach; *Cinematographer:* Dev Jennings; *Editor:* Richard Currier; *Cast:* Thelma Todd, ZaSu Pitts, Charles Judels, Allan Lane, Guinn "Big Boy" Williams, Stuart Holmes, Carrie Daumery, Harry Schultz, Charlie Hall, Blanche Payson, Adrienne D'Ambricourt, William J. O'Brien, William Yetter, Sr.; *Released by* MGM on November 14, 1931; Two Reels

Military comedy was already something of a staple, or perhaps even a cliché, by the time Thelma Todd and ZaSu Pitts made *War Mamas*, their fourth two-reel comedy together. As far back as the silent era, comedians in the service would find themselves behind enemy lines and have to use comically creative ideas to extricate themselves. Such is the framework for *War Mamas*.

World War I ambulance drivers Thelma and ZaSu get sidetracked while bringing back a couple of soldiers from the front (actually their boyfriends, who have stowed away in their vehicle). They end up in enemy territory, disguise themselves as a couple of German fräuleins, and engage in a strip poker game with two enemy soldiers. Winning the game and stripping the Germans of their uniforms, Thelma and ZaSu are able to escape and return to their allies.

Having the girls play ambulance drivers might be an underlying connection to Ernest Hemingway, who performed that service in the military during World War I. By the time this 1931 comedy was produced, Hemingway had written extensively about his exploits in books like *A Farewell to Arms*, which was new and popular at this time, already a stage play and would be filmed as a movie the following year.

War Mamas is a very funny comedy that is filled with gags. An early comic bit has Thelma struggling to help ZaSu off with her too-tight boots (a situation that was used for the entire length of an earlier Laurel and Hardy short, 1930's *Be Big*). When she pulls, the force knocks ZaSu back into a table, which causes a large ceramic pot to fall out the window. This happens twice, once for each boot, the pot first shattering over a bugler, and then the girls' tough sergeant.

It is also interesting right away to see how army comedy clichés are altered when women play the lead roles. While the typical tough sergeant is in place (played by the familiar and welcome comic heavy Blanche Payson), one of the very first visuals features a male soldier sneaking out of a window and kissing a hand goodbye, introducing a sexual angle that would likely not otherwise be there. This is expanded upon a short time later when a cannon's explosive power causes the barracks to shake, the floor under ZaSu and Thelma's bed to give away, and the girls plummeting into the bed of two male soldiers below. Of course the sergeant walks in and gets the wrong idea. It is

Left to right: Allan Lane, Guinn "Big Boy" Williams, ZaSu Pitts, Thelma Todd and Carrie Daumery in *War Mamas* (1931).

likely the pre–Code status of this short is what allowed the sexual content. This is not only the aforementioned gags, but also the later strip poker scene where women, who know the game, manage to handily defeat the amateurs repeatedly and soon have divested each soldier of his uniform.

Once the central idea is established, and the girls are lost in their ambulance and find themselves behind enemy lines, Thelma and ZaSu end up at a posh party where a German woman kindly introduces them as her nieces in order to keep them out of trouble. Director Marshall Neilan creatively uses existing MGM sets.. Their American soldier boyfriends are hiding in the cellar until one goes to get help while the other remains. Thelma, who speaks German, lures enemy soldiers, one by one, into the cellar where her boyfriend knocks them out. Meanwhile, ZaSu pretends to be very drunk in order to entice another soldier. It is then that they are talked into the strip poker game. Once the soldiers are stripped, they are locked in a closet and Thelma dons one of the uniforms while her boyfriend takes over a car, and the three of them drive away as the movie ends.

Overall, *War Mamas* is amusing and it further establishes the girls as a team, but it is still a bit uneven and disjointed. The opening gags at the base are good slapstick fun, establishing the sergeant as a comic heavy, a couple of boyfriends, and the sexual premise accompanying a pre–Code movie about men and women stationed on the same military base. But the central theme leaves all of that behind once Thelma and ZaSu go behind enemy lines. And when ZaSu's boyfriend (again played by Guinn "Big Boy" Williams) escapes to get help, he is not heard from again, providing a loose end. The film ends rather abruptly.

ZaSu once again mentions missing her hometown of Joplin in this film like she had in a previous one, further building up her character by giving a possible reason for her naivety and nervousness; she is someone from a small town thrust into unfamiliar situations, while Thelma is more worldly and has to help her along. But whether it was for show or not, her character appeared almost too flattered by the German soldier's attentions. The poker scene was amusing but a bit overlong.

War Mamas was well received. *Film Daily* called it "pleasantly diverting pretty much all the way through"[7] while *Motion Picture Herald* indicated that "an audience at a New York neighborhood house extracted numerous laughs from the nonsense of the two feminine players."[8]

Hal Roach had a reputation for experimenting with the pairing of actors and observing how the teaming worked over several films. His most noted success was with Laurel and Hardy. But he had also attempted to co-star Harold Lloyd and Snub Pollard during the silent era (although they often played adversaries) and we've already mentioned the teaming of Thelma Todd and Charley Chase that was so cohesive, Chase wanted to make it permanent.

So perhaps putting Todd and Pitts in the typical framework of a military comedy was part of this experiment. There is a typical premise, some fun gags, and good performances from both comediennes who further exhibit their effectiveness as a team. And everyone gets a better understanding of where they can go with this teaming. A formula would settle in after a few films, and things would pick up as the series tried the talents of different directors who could add more to the proceedings with their visions. Michelle Morgan stated in her book *The Ice Cream Blonde*:

> They shared a fearless commitment to the rough-and-tumble nature of slapstick. When the scripts called for them to end up neck-deep in river water or be thrown around the dance floor by partners with two left feet, they took it all in stride. When their clothes ended up messy and often torn, they didn't complain. But they didn't take themselves too seriously, either; they'd often spoil scenes due to their inability to keep a straight face, then have to avoid eye contact with each other lest the uncontrollable laughter start back up again.[9]

On the Loose (1931)

Directed by Hal Roach; *Dialogue by* H.M. Walker; *Produced by* Hal Roach; *Cinematographer:* Len Powers; *Editor:* Richard Currier; *Cast:* Thelma Todd, ZaSu Pitts, John Loder, Claud Allister, Billy Gilbert, Gordon Douglas, Charlie Hall, Dorothy Layton, Estelle Etterre, Buddy McDonald, Jack Hill, Stan Laurel, Oliver Hardy; *Released by* MGM on December 26, 1931; Two Reels

On the Loose might be the best-known Thelma Todd–ZaSu Pitts two-reeler, mostly due to Stan Laurel and Oliver Hardy's cameo as the film's closing gag. There was a certain camaraderie among Roach players, and since Laurel and Hardy were the most popular comedians on the lot, they would sometimes appear in others' films in surprise cameos that would delight movie-goers. Laurel and Hardy appeared as babies in the Our Gang short *Wild Poses*. They showed up as hitchhikers in the Charley Chase two-reeler *On the Wrong Trek*. And they appear with Thelma and ZaSu in *On the Loose*.

Before filming *On the Loose*, Todd appeared in director Roland West's dramatic feature *Corsair*. West wanted to groom Thelma as a top dramatic actress, something she craved. To distance her from her two-reel comedies, West suggested she change her screen name to Alison Loyd. So, in *Corsair*, Thelma is billed as Alison Loyd. Thelma told columnist Dan Thomas:

> I have always wanted to play dramatic roles, but you know how it is out here. Casting directors have a way of keeping players in a certain groove and never letting them out. Once you make a good impression in a certain type of role, there is practically no chance of getting away from it. Everyone has always thought of Thelma Todd as a rowdy comedienne. She never could get an opportunity to do anything else. But, as Alison Loyd, I at least have a chance of being disassociated from my past roles. If I happen to score a success in *Corsair*, I am sure my new name will identify me with dramatic roles. Yet, even after establishing myself as a dramatic actress, should a comedy role come along that I want to play, I at least will be able to get some consideration because of the years I spent as a comedienne.[10]

Hal Roach reportedly stated that he didn't care how she chose to be billed in movies outside of his studio, but whenever she appeared in a Hal Roach production, she would continue to be billed as Thelma Todd. However, the new moniker was short-lived. *Corsair* was not a success and Roland West left filmmaking, planning to perhaps return in the late 1930s.

ZaSu Pitts and Thelma Todd in *On the Loose* (1931).

Meanwhile, ZaSu, who had already established herself in drama before doing the comedies with Thelma, continued to work in more serious features between shorts. Before starting *On the Loose,* she appeared in the Columbia mystery *The Secret Witness.*

On the Loose deals with dating from the female perspective. During this era, the man would invariably choose where the date would take place and pay for everything. Thelma and ZaSu always seem to meet up with guys who take them to Coney Island until they are simply sick of it. There is some amusing dialogue at the outset when they come home from yet another date at Coney:

> THELMA: Well, that's one more—and the last one!
> ZaSu: The last what?
> THELMA: My last trip to—Coney Island!
> ZaSu: I should hope so. I could smell hot dogs for a week after I come away from that place. And those merry-go-rounds! I know the pedigree of every wooden horse in the place.
> THELMA: What do we go there for anyway? We can get the same effect by staying at home and hitting ourselves on the head with a hammer.

They later meet two Englishmen who ask them on a date. Dressed up in new outfits that the Englishmen bought them, Thelma and ZaSu are shocked to discover they've once again been taken to Coney Island. The Brits truly enjoy the various activities such as a fun house, a shooting gallery and a roller-coaster, while a bored Thelma and ZaSu walk through indifferently, nodding to workers whom they seem to know well. Thelma shocks her date by handily outdoing him at the shooting gallery with a smaller gun. The girls know how to keep their dresses from shooting up when the air hits them on the floor of the fun house. In another amusing scene, Thelma gets a little boy's lollipop stuck under her dress going down a slide, and the boy actually goes up under her dress to get it back. There's a lot of innuendo in this film that probably wouldn't have been allowed had it been made a few years later.

The Englishmen remain completely oblivious to the fact that the girls don't appear to be having a good time as Thelma and ZaSu grit their teeth and persevere.

The film explores the idea that the men, both the Englishmen and the men implied in the opening dialogue, don't take the women's feelings into account when choosing activities, but still expect them to go along with them.

The stock shots of an actual amusement park circa 1931 have a cultural-

Left to right: ZaSu Pitts, Thelma Todd, John Loder and Claud Allister in *On the Loose* (1931).

historical interest in the 21st century. Each activity has some solid comic potential. There is a running gag where a woman with a bullying jealous boyfriend keeps stumbling into the arms of one of the Englishmen. When the boyfriend starts to get tough, Thelma steps in and punches him. The dynamic between Thelma and ZaSu is not as pronounced here. Usually Thelma is savvy and ZaSu is the bewildered innocent. This time they are more of a team, as one, in their reaction to Coney Island and the men who take them.

While John Loder and Claud Allister are amusing enough as the English suitors, Billy Gilbert is even funnier as a prissy dress salesman. He is too embarrassed to properly describe the way his fashions fit across certain parts of the female body, much to the amusement of his female customers. He flits about daintily while waiting on customers, but when he is alone with his models he changes to a boorish, "Youse dames get out there!" But the biggest laugh from supporting characters comes at the end when Stan Laurel and Oliver Hardy show up in their unbilled cameo, asking the girls on a date to Coney Island! Thelma and ZaSu respond by throwing their Coney Island mementos at the fleeing duo in a very funny conclusion.[11]

Transcending beyond their gender roles in several scenes, while maintaining the gender identity of the era, Thelma and ZaSu continued to explore avenues in slapstick comedy that still resonate in the 21st century. *On the Loose* is one of their funniest films up to this point. It's notoriety due to the Laurel and Hardy cameo allows for one of their better movies to also be one of their better known.

Upon completing this comedy, ZaSu Pitts went to Universal where she was appearing in another team dynamic, opposite Slim Summerville, in the feature *The Unexpected Father*. She had a smaller role as a maid in the Lionel Barrymore vehicle *Broken Lullaby* at Paramount. These jobs outside of the Roach studio were helpful to ZaSu's interest in expanding her acting career.

Sealskins (1932)

Directed by Morey Lightfoot, Gilbert Pratt; *Dialogue by* H.M. Walker; *Produced by* Hal Roach; *Cinematographer:* Len Powers; *Editor:* Richard Currier; *Cast:* Thelma Todd, ZaSu Pitts, Charlie Hall, Leo Willis, Billy Gilbert, Buddy McDonald, Frank Austin, Charles Gemora, Eddie Baker, Clifford Thompson, Harry Earles; *Released by* MGM on February 6, 1932; Two Reels

It was inevitable that Thelma and ZaSu would end up in a haunted house comedy, and *Sealskins* is it. Just as we discussed in the *War Mamas* chapter that military comedy had already become a staple in screen comedy, so is horror comedy.

The haunted house concept had been a staple of screen comedies since the silent era (explored with special brilliance by Buster Keaton in his appropriately titled 1921 two-reeler *The Haunted House*). It must have seemed, on paper, that putting a female comedy team in a scare comedy was a perfect set-up.

The premise for *Sealskins* has Thelma, a newspaper office typist, come across a story about a valuable seal from Siberia being stolen. It is a piece of jewelry, but when Thelma gets a tip about an aquatic seal taken from the circus, she pursues that case, with her friend ZaSu being asked to tag along.

It is difficult to avoid clichés in a genre pairing like horror and comedy, as it is pretty much as old as cinema itself. As a result, *Sealskins* often relies a bit too much on mechanical gags regarding creepy inhabitants of an old dark house, a stormy night, dummies mistaken for real people, a gorilla and other decidedly standard ideas. But this sort of structure still manages to work effectively here. What makes this film amusing is Thelma and ZaSu's reactions and responses to the execution of each of these standard ideas.

Despite most of the humor being pretty basic, there's some nice suspense built up in a couple of the scenes following the girls around the house. One notably amusing sequence occurs when Thelma and ZaSu go into a closet and we hear a scuffle and protests from ZaSu. Moments later Thelma emerges with her friend's undergarment slip, using it to wrap the seal up and disguise it as a baby. Risqué, but in this pre–Code comedy, it got past the censors. Such a gag would not likely be possible when the Production Code was more vigorously enforced after 1934.

Sealskins offers a slightly different take on the Thelma–ZaSu relationship. Thelma seems more impulsive, her desire to be a reporter and impress her boss trumping her usual sound reasoning as she takes off in pursuit of this seal. ZaSu, while still timid, is more the voice of reason, and goes along in order to keep Thelma from going too far, from taking dangerous risks for the sake of career advancement. The house is inhabited by sideshow characters who aren't bad people,

Left to right: ZaSu Pitts, Clifford Thompson and Thelma Todd in *Sealskins* (1932).

31

but their strange appearance alone is startling enough to the girls, who are already on edge in the creepy surroundings.

Sealskins concludes when Thelma summons her newspaper boss to the scene, indicating she has the seal, and getting fired when it turns out to be quite different than what was expected. As Thelma and ZaSu retrieve their coats, Thelma says, "I guess there ain't nothing else gonna happen." The girls then see a gorilla and burst through a door to escape.

The director of *Sealskins*, Gilbert Pratt, was a veteran, but had little experience at Roach Studios, having only helmed the Charley Chase short *Hasty Marriage* the year before. Since Chase generally supervised his own movies, Pratt likely did little with the creative process and his set-ups and shot selections were based on Chase's vision to a greater degree than his own. Pratt's real talents had been exhibited during the silent era. He directed such comedians as Stan Laurel (*Mud and Sand*) and Harold Lloyd (*The Non-Stop Kid*) as well as everyone from Lloyd Hamilton to the Ton of Fun Trio. Pratt, therefore, responded well to the mechanical gags that were as old as silent comedy. Also a writer, Pratt provided stories for Laurel and Hardy (their 1940 feature *Saps at Sea*) as well as a couple of Three Stooges shorts at Columbia later in the 1940s. His co-director, Morely Lightfoot, was a prop man. This is the only film for which Lightfoot is credited with direction.

The cast is filled out nicely, not only with Hal Roach stalwarts Charlie Hall and Billy Gilbert, but also offbeat characters like diminutive Harry Earles and eight-foot giant Clifford Thompson. Earles had appeared in both the silent and sound versions of *The Unholy Three*, and at the time of *Sealskins* he was also seen in the notorious MGM feature *Freaks*. Thompson, a famous novelty attraction, remains noted as the tallest man to ever appear in a movie. When he got older and needed a cane to get around, he stopped touring and making movies to study law, later becoming the world's tallest lawyer.

Film Daily liked this short, saying it had "a wealth of funny situations with some clever dialogue with which to work. The girls have turned out one of the biggest laugh numbers in this series. It's a surefire laugh number." *Variety*, however, dismissed it as "one of the less attractive comedies made by the exasperated ZaSu Pitts and the beauteous Thelma Todd."

It was around this time that Todd met and hired Mae Whitehead, an African-American woman whose childhood had been riddled with racism. Whitehead saw her house burned down by neighbors who did not want her family to live nearby. She had to be walked to school, for her own protection, by her mother, who'd sit in the back of the classroom quietly knitting. Mae

Left to right: ZaSu Pitts, Charles Gemora and Thelma Todd in *Sealskins* (1932).

traveled to Los Angeles to find domestic work possibly in the wealthy film community. Thelma hired her as a maid and supportive companion, a job Whitehead had for the remainder of Thelma's life.

With Whitehead effectively handling a lot of Thelma's everyday life, the actress had more time for social events that helped promote her films. She and ZaSu reportedly attended parties together, were spotted out shopping and going to lunch, and there were even apocryphal stories in the trade press (such as claiming they took jobs as waitresses and got fired as research for one of their comedies). These stories helped bolster the fact that, along with being partnered on-screen, Thelma and ZaSu were also very close friends off-screen.

After the release of *Sealskins*, Thelma next co-starred with Ben Lyon in the Columbia feature *The Big Timer*. After that she was back at Roach to support old friend Charley Chase in his two-reeler *The Nickel Nurser*. It was the last time she and Chase worked in a movie together. ZaSu, meanwhile, took a role in Universal's feature *Steady Company* starring Norman Foster and directed by Edward Ludwig (aka Edward I. Luddy).

33

Red Noses (1932)

Directed by James W. Horne; *Dialogue by* H.M. Walker; *Produced by* Hal Roach; *Cinematographer:* Art Lloyd; *Editor:* Richard Currier; *Cast:* Thelma Todd, ZaSu Pitts, Blanche Payson, Wilfred Lucas, Frank Terry, Billy Gilbert, Lyle Tayo, Bobby Burns, Germaine De Neel, Dorothy Layton, Estelle Etterre; *Released by* MGM on March 19, 1932; Two Reels; *Working title: The Sniffles*; *Reissue title: Ladies in a Turkish Bath*

Red Noses is another one of the better known Thelma Todd–ZaSu Pitts comedies, due to its being available to the home collector market for many years during the pre-video era. Blackhawk Films, a distributor of 8mm and 16mm films for the home collector, had the non-theatrical sales rights to *Red Noses,* as well almost all of Roach's Laurel and Hardy and Our Gang films and several of the Charley Chase comedies. As a result, *Red Noses* was among the comedies run at film festivals in the 1960s and 1970s.

Perhaps the rowdiest comedy that Thelma and ZaSu had made thus far, *Red Noses* is also one of their funniest. The girls are suffering from bad colds and can't go to work on a day when the firm desperately needs them. Their boss promises a bonus and a raise if they come in, and arranges for a Turkish bath to give them a treatment that will cure their colds in an hour. Once they are in the health center, Thelma and ZaSu are put through a series of outrageous treatments including bucking chairs, fast-paced treadmills, massage treatments that seem like wrestling matches, and a mud treatment that ends up in a mud fight. ZaSu steals a man's suit of clothes in an attempt to escape, resulting in a wild slapstick chase.

This is the only Todd–Pitts short directed by James Horne, one of the Roach Studio's better directors (he later directed a short featuring Thelma and Patsy Kelly). Horne understood a cinematic method known as *mise en scène*, which is a French term that deals with how props are arranged on stage. In film, it deals with how objects are placed within the frame. In the first scene that features the girls, Horne has them sharing a bed (quite a necessity during the Depression) while their room is strewn with a hot water bottle, a tub in which the girls could soak their feet (with newspapers seen beneath it), discarded handkerchiefs and other such debris. It creates a good atmosphere to help enhance the actresses' performances. Thelma is disgruntled by the inconvenience and simply wants to be left alone to rest. ZaSu is typically forlorn and suffering.

It is interesting how each of the women is treated by others. When ZaSu answers the boss' phone call, he angrily shouts into the phone. When he does so again and discovers it is Thelma now on the line, he backs down and speaks in a friendlier manner. This gives the impression that he feels like he can walk all over ZaSu, but Thelma is less likely to let him boss her around unfairly, so he needs to have a calmer and kinder demeanor so she doesn't fly off the handle as well.

The film's transition from this set-up into the health club reveals another factor in how the women are presented. When they change into their workout gear, Thelma is clad in a tight, revealing top, while ZaSu wears a sweatshirt that is too big for her. The film plays it as ZaSu being comically too bashful for more revealing workout clothes, but it stands to reason that the film's intention is to play up Thelma's sexiness.

ZaSu's immediate reaction to being offered a Turkish bath is amusing: "No Turk is going to give me a bath!" When they arrive at the health club (holding handkerchiefs the size of dish towels), the French proprietor accidentally calls ZaSu "Miss Spitz." She soon afterward sneezes into some powder. This scene concludes with some rather bizarre comedy. The girls see a woman being wheeled out on a stretcher, and overhear she's had a heart attack after undergoing "treatment 37." So when the girls are told they are getting "treatment 27," ZaSu gets the wrong idea and yells, "No, no, that's the heart attack." Their health coach assures them "no, that's 37," as if a heart attack was a perfectly appropriate outcome to that particular treatment.

The rough slapstick starts up when Thelma is jerked about in a chair, while ZaSu is jostled around on a riding contraption, each of the girls laughing at the other's predicament but protesting their own. The treadmill follows, and while these bits are superficially amusing, they are mechanical and don't allow the girls to do much more than react. The treadmill is shown going in fast motion, which might have enhanced the gag in 1932 but doesn't hold up as well in the 21st century with our more advanced special effects. The only really good laugh during this sequence is when the treadmill propels ZaSu across the floor onto a stretcher, which topples and knocks a woman to the floor. The woman screams and ZaSu states, "What are you hollering about, look where I came from?"

Since 1932 is a pre–Code year, there is a great deal of sexual innuendo throughout the health club sequences (the line "Girls, take off your clothes" is used as a direction several times). When they first do so, ZaSu sees a bulge sticking through a curtain that is obviously Thelma's bottom. She gently pats it and says, "Is that you, Thelma?" Thelma angrily responds, "Now who else would it be?" The massage scene between Thelma and Amazonian Blanche Payson ends with them wrestling and tussling on the floor, the contrast with slender, shapely Thelma and large hulking Payson adding a neat visual to the scene. Meanwhile, the middle-aged, heavyset Lyle Tayo plays the woman giving ZaSu her massage, stroking her arm, caressing her neck, even using a vibrator about her body and causing her to react with ticklish giggling.

The mud fight begins when ZaSu walks in as Thelma is getting a mud-pack, and believes her friend is being attacked. She picks up some mud and flings it at Payson, and soon this escalates, extending to the outer area where a haughty woman is hit, ruining her expensive dress. The girls are ordered to leave.

For most of the health club scenes, there is a running gag where Thelma and ZaSu simply want to get dressed and leave, but they cannot find their clothes. When ZaSu is wiping mud from her face, she accidentally walks out of the health club and into a tailor shop in the same building. She steals a man's clothes and attempts to escape, but only causes a panic as she returns to the health club, and is mistaken by several women in towels for an intruding man.

This wild slapstick conclusion includes a wonderful performance by Billy Gilbert as the man in the tailor's office. His reaction to seeing, in the mirror, his clothes walking out on another person, is funny enough, but then he gives chase while having to hold up his semi-tailored pants. He wrestles with ZaSu as his pants are falling down, while Thelma jumps on his back and starts pulling his hair.

The girls finally do escape, with Thelma still wrapped in a towel as "the woman" while the suit-clad ZaSu is "the man." The film's final scene features the two of them walking down a crowded street, trying to maintain enough composure to not be noticed.

Along with the rather blatant sexual innuendo, the roughhouse slapstick and the dated technical methods to enhance some gags (even the final shot is done in front of a process screen), *Red Noses* is perhaps the most fascinating Todd–Pitts short up to this point. Most of it holds up nicely.

After *Red Noses*, Thelma secured a good role at Paramount in Frank Tuttle's *This Is the Night*, in which a young Cary Grant made his film debut. Meanwhile, ZaSu went to Columbia and supported Barbara Stanwyck in *Shopworn*, and then had a supporting part in Universal's *Destry Rides Again*, a Tom Mix Western which has nothing to do with the 1939 classic featuring James Stewart and Marlene Dietrich. However, it is noted for being Mix's first talkie, and his first movie in three years.

Strictly Unreliable (1932)

Directed by George Marshall; *Dialogue by* H.M. Walker; *Produced by* Hal Roach; *Cinematographer:* Len Powers; *Editor:* Richard Currier; *Cast:* Thelma Todd, ZaSu Pitts, Charlotte Mineau, Bud Jamison, Billy Gilbert, Charlie Hall, Symona Boniface, Charles Williams; *Released by* MGM on April 28, 1932; Two Reels

It seems fitting that Thelma and ZaSu would do a short comedy about being in show business, and *Strictly Unreliable* is constructed from that premise. Curiously, this is also less of a team effort. It plays more as a ZaSu Pitts solo comedy with Thelma Todd in support.

The film is something of a period piece as it depicts "show folk" staying in a boarding house, which was rather common back in the days of vaudeville. ZaSu is a housekeeper at one of these houses, presenting herself as the curious outsider who is fascinated by the various acts. Thelma is one of those acts, but she has not worked in a while. When she does finally get a job, which is to begin at a local theater that night, the landlady puts her out of her room due to non-payment of rent, and will not allow her to retrieve her belongings until at least some of the back rent has been paid. Meanwhile the landlady's out-of-work actor brother moves into Thelma's room. ZaSu is enlisted to retrieve Thelma's things (she needs them for the show), and then goes to the theater where Thelma is to start work with her act. At the theater, ZaSu stumbles into a series of different vaudeville performances, culminating in her making a shambles of Thelma's act.

The fact that this comedy centers almost completely on ZaSu, with Thelma in the same support as the landlady (Charlotte Mineau, credited as the phonetic Meno in the credits) and her brother (Bud Jamison), gives this film a somewhat different vibe. Most of ZaSu's comic business is done without another person to play off of, and is central to the proceedings of each scene.

The film opens with ZaSu looking through the keyhole of a room where a contortionist is rehearsing. Fascinated, she tries to copy the movements and ends up tangling herself up in knots. This opening effectively introduces her innocent interest and bumbling nature. The way the scene is shot is an effective use of the cinematic process. A leg bends up by ZaSu's face. Obviously it is not actually her leg, but keeping it a medium shot so we can't see the trick makes it a funny visual.

Meanwhile, Thelma's inability to get into her room without paying some of the rent she owes is a real problem as she can't go on that night without her costumes. That is the conflict that is central to the short's narrative.

Bud Jamison is all blustery hamminess as the landlady's unsuccessful actor brother, taking over the room unbeknownst to ZaSu, who enters to get Thelma's things while Bud is in the bathroom. She must maneuver to avoid both him and the landlady and still get the costumes. Director George Marshall does a good job of cutting between all of these central characters moving about from place to place, as ZaSu and Thelma try to go about their task without being caught. Eventually Thelma is in the room without Bud realizing it. She hides in the closet. ZaSu goes in to get Thelma's things, accidentally

Left to right: ZaSu Pitts, Thelma Todd and Bud Jamison in *Strictly Unreliable* (1932).

grabs Bud's baggage and hides in the same closet. Bud comes out and, thinking that his suitcase has been stolen, complains loudly to the landlady. The girls reveal themselves and manage to escape by shoving the landlady into the closet, and hitting Bud in the stomach and kicking him in the shin. As Thelma and ZaSu hurry to the theater, Bud and the landlady follow.

On paper it appears that there is more of a team dynamic here than what appears on screen. But, as mentioned earlier in the chapter, Thelma offers no more support than either Bud Jamison or Charlotte Mineau in this scene. While ZaSu is responding to a request by Thelma, and does attend the theater with her, that is only to establish their connection. Once at the theater, Thelma again is missing from the action as it centers on ZaSu. It is not long before ZaSu inadvertently wanders on stage during a drawing room drama being acted out before an audience. During a dramatic conflict, there is a struggle for the actor's gun and the actress is killed. ZaSu, believing it is all for real, rushes to the actress, who gets up and says, "Get off the stage, you fool!" getting a laugh from the audience. ZaSu then realizes it is an act and is relieved. The actor tries to keep things going by saying "No witnesses!" and shoving ZaSu off the stage. The act then continues, with the actress trying to cover for the intrusion, but ZaSu ends up on stage again, not only ruining the act but getting hooked onto a curtain as it is raised. High above the stage when an acrobatic act comes on after the drama, ZaSu ends up in a top chair during a balancing routine. The scene is done with stunt people, director Marshall cutting from close-up reactions of ZaSu to a medium shot presenting what is happening on stage, keeping the edits tight enough to make it appear that ZaSu is indeed that high up.

This idea is extended when ZaSu ends up in the dressing room of several chorus girls. Mistaken as one of them, ZaSu is put into a costume, pushed out on stage, and finds herself hooked onto a stage rope. She then swings across the stage as Thelma tries to go on. An added dynamic to the proceedings has the landlady and Bud in pursuit of both girls. When Bud ends up onstage with ZaSu swinging about, and the two start struggling, Thelma sees an opportunity and starts playing the piano. Bud, also seeing an opportunity when the audience laughs and applauds at the antics, goes into a purposeful Apache dance and mutters to ZaSu to play along, because they're "a hit." Despite the effectiveness of their "performance," ZaSu has had enough and when the manager offers her 40 weeks to continue doing the same act, she starts choking him. "Okay," he gasps as the film concludes, "I'll give you 50 weeks!"

Strictly Unreliable is quite outrageous and amusing, really giving ZaSu the spotlight as the center of all the comedy. Bud Jamison, already a veteran whose career dated back to Charlie Chaplin's Essanay period, is amusing in support. Charlotte Mineau appeared in many of Chaplin's brilliant Mutual productions. This was her penultimate film, although she lived through the 1970s.

Bud Jamison might be best known for his work in the 1930s and 1940s with the Three Stooges, playing everything from a comic heavy to a comic foil for the trio. Thus, it is especially interesting to find, as the actress in the drawing room drama, Symona Boniface, whose best work was with the Stooges, often as a haughty dowager (the same type of character Margaret Dumont played for the Marx Brothers). The supporting cast also includes a lot of funny moments with Billy Gilbert hamming it up as the dramatic actor and Charlie Hall as a harried stage manager.

One misses the team dynamic in *Strictly Unreliable*, and the pairing works better when ZaSu has someone like the more reasonable Thelma around to keep her grounded. But *Strictly Unreliable* is still funny and effective and did allow ZaSu to show off her full range of comedic talents.

Prior to the next Todd–Pitts comedy *The Old Bull*, ZaSu was busy in three feature films: a Fox courtroom drama, *The Trial of Vivienne Ware*, the low-budget indie *Strangers of the Evening*, a quirky murder mystery, and the romantic drama *Westward Passage* featuring a young Laurence Olivier plus Bonita Granville in her film debut. ZaSu continued to flourish in roles outside of the series, being allowed to play a variety of different roles.

ZaSu liked Hal Roach and had become close friends with Thelma, but still she was already losing interest in doing the short comedies. ZaSu she felt these less prestigious productions kept her away from doing more feature work. She also started to become weary at the physical demands of the slapstick comedy required in the Roach comedies. She was currently under contract and, as a professional, planned to give her best performance in each movie. But she pondered what she wanted to do with her career, and how she wanted to approach cinematic opportunities. While she appreciated the creative freedom that Hal Roach allowed, she didn't know if two-reelers were where she wanted to expend this much energy.

The Old Bull (1932)

Directed by George Marshall; *Dialogue by* H.M. Walker; *Produced by* Hal Roach; *Cinematographer:* Art Lloyd; *Editor:* Richard Currier; *Cast:*

Thelma Todd, ZaSu Pitts, Otto Fries, Bobby Burns, Ham Kinsey; *Shooting days:* March 18–25, 1932; *Released by* MGM on June 4, 1932; Two Reels

While the previous film *Strictly Unreliable* gave much more attention to ZaSu, with Thelma in support, *The Old Bull* is a team effort filled with amusing comic ideas, along with some very dated technology.

The Old Bull starts abruptly, with Thelma and ZaSu pulled over on the side of a country road. ZaSu insists she be allowed to drive for a while. The girls struggle as ZaSu tries to move into the driver's seat over Thelma who is moving toward the passenger side. Once ZaSu is behind the wheel, there is a wild slapstick scene where she loses control of the car and crashes into a farm, disrupting its livestock and crops. The farmer orders them off his property, keeping the car as collateral for the damage they caused. The women go wandering about, lost in the country, until they are so tired they knock on the next house they come to, only to discover it is the farm they had just left.

Left to right: **Thelma Todd, ZaSu Pitts and director George Marshall on the set of** *The Old Bull* **(1932).**

They walked around for miles in a circle! When they try sneaking their car out of the barn, they are confronted by a lion that has escaped from a nearby circus.

The Old Bull is noteworthy as having likely been influenced by two Laurel and Hardy subjects filmed only months earlier and released right around the same time. First, *County Hospital* features a climactic car chase that is done with rear projection that looks quite phony by modern-day standards (but was a big hit with less discerning audiences of 1932). Second, the loose lion idea was used in the Laurel and Hardy comedy *The Chimp*. While both ideas fit comfortably enough within the context of a Todd–Pitts short, their inclusion does show how ideas in Roach films could inspire use in different films.

The car chase during the early portion of the film is done with the same phony process screen technique as found in the Laurel and Hardy movie. And, as with the Laurel and Hardy comedy, it was also enjoyed by period audiences. Unlike the scene in *County Hospital,* which benefits from a rousing musical score and quick edits, the *Old Bull* scene is less effective as it does not contain any music nor rapid editing. It does feature several cutaways of an actual car driving recklessly through a farm setting, which helps a bit. While this scene with the car out of control got big laughs in 1932, it looks pretty fake in the 21st century.

A scene like this is still interesting despite the fact that it no longer has the same impact it might have enjoyed in earlier years. Our appreciation of film history allows us to be more fascinated by this more primitive use of special effects. This is not to say that all chase scenes were presented in this manner. There are well-staged, authentic chase scenes as far back as the silent era. But the budget, the technology immediately available, and the amount of time were obviously all factors involved in filming this scene (and the one in *County Hospital*) in such a manner. That it remained effective to period audiences is part of the interest (and perhaps curiosity).

There is some amusing dialogue when the car finally crashes through the barn and the girls are buried under bales of hay. The angry farmer states, "You ran right through the door!" and ZaSu responds, "Well, the door wasn't open!" As he helps ZaSu get her foot free from the car (causing her to push Thelma's face into the steering wheel and make the horn blare), she opens a grain hatch and makes an even bigger mess. The farmer insists on keeping the car to pay for the damage, and that is how Thelma and ZaSu end up wandering the desolate country area alone at night. Much of the opening footage of *The Old Bull* deals with struggling. The girls struggle to change seats in

42

the car, struggle to avoid danger while it is out of control, struggle to extricate themselves when it crashes.

The amusing dialogue continues once the girls arrive at the same house after miles of walking. When the farmer comes to the door, they register surprise and then ZaSu asks, "Did you move?" He slams the door on them and (similar to a scene in the Laurel and Hardy silent *Big Business*) ZaSu finds that her dress is caught in the door. She tries to remove herself from it, when the farmer opens the door again, freeing her, and knocking helpful Thelma out of the scene, in a slapstick gag that is remarkable for its timing and execution.

After a report of a lion escaped from a traveling circus comes over the radio, the film separates the girls and gives them each their own solo comedy scenes. ZaSu goes into the barn to try getting the car out, while Thelma stays near the house holding a can with a rope through it (when the role is pulled, the sound is similar to a lion's roar). This keeps the farmer inside, fearful that the escaped lion is on the premises. While ZaSu fumbles about the darkness in the barn, upsetting a cow and some pigs, Thelma sneaks around with the noisemaker, only to notice the actual lion on the premises.

Finally, the girls get their car and are ready to escape, when they are stopped by the farmer. The lion is then discovered to be in the back seat. The farmer runs away, but ZaSu once again has her foot caught, so they frantically try to extricate her as the lion roars behind them.

It is beneficial to this short that Thelma and ZaSu are again working as a unit. Their camaraderie really shines, right from that opening scene of them struggling to switch seats in the car. They continue to appear very comfortable working together, which helps make their chemistry and their scenes together even more amusing.

As indicated, the 1932 effects didn't age well, but there is enough comedy to sustain *The Old Bull*, and it was hailed as one of the duo's best so far upon its release. A May 7, 1932, *Motion Picture Herald* review stated, "There are some real laughs in this comedy."[12] The May 5, 1932, *Film Daily* said it had "plenty of slapstick [and] fast direction to hold up a satisfactory tempo."[13] The October 4, 1932, *Variety* called it "very funny," praised its "many novel laugh situations" and recommended it as "worth buying for any program."[14] Finally, a theater owner writing to *Motion Picture Herald* in its New Year's Eve 1932 issue called *The Old Bull* "one continuous scream."

Otto Fries, who plays the farmer, had been appearing in Roach productions since the silent era, including films with Our Gang, Laurel and Hardy and Charley Chase. This was not his first film with Thelma and ZaSu, nor would it be his last He continued to appear in Roach movies until his death in 1938. As the farm hands, Bobby Burns and Ham Kinsey extend the small supporting cast. Burns was also in several Roach comedies, sometimes only in seconds-long bits doing a pratfall (his flip while hosing down the lawn in Laurel and Hardy's *Helpmates* is a good example). Ham Kinsey also had small roles in many Roach productions, but is perhaps better noted as Stan Laurel's double/stuntman in several films.

After finishing this short, Thelma and ZaSu kept busy during the Hal Roach Studios' annual shutdown, which usually occurred over March and April. Beforehand, however, the women signed new contracts for more two-reel comedies. A blurb in the March 22 *Variety* stated:

> Thelma Todd and ZaSu Pitts have been given contracts for three shorts to be made on Hal Roach's program for the next year. Options for the additional three in the series of six announced. Miss Todd will go to Paramount during the Roach shutdown to appear in the Four Marx Brothers' *Horse Feathers*.[15]

Left to right: Thelma's maid Mae Whitehead, ZaSu Pitts and Thelma Todd on the set of *The Old Bull* (1932).

Thelma's performance as the college widow in *Horse Feathers* remains one of her finest. She does a delightful musical number with Chico, is serenaded by a smitten Harpo, and has some especially funny scenes with Groucho. In one scene, she falls out of a canoe and asks that Groucho throw her a life saver; he tosses a piece of candy by that name rather than a preserver.

Next, Thelma was back at MGM for what may be Buster Keaton's best sound feature, *Speak Easily,* which also featured Jimmy Durante. Thelma is delightful as the female lead in this comedy, and performs well with both leading comedians. Her character is that of an actress who will do whatever is necessary to get ahead, so she makes a play for wealthy milquetoast Keaton. The two do a drunk bit together that is one of the highlights of the film.

The busy ZaSu made appearances in the films *Is My Face Red, Make Me a Star, Roar of the Dragon* and *The Vanishing Frontier.* ZaSu remained dedicated to her craft as an actress, and took on as many varied roles as she could.

Show Business (1932)

Directed by Jules White; *Dialogue by* H.M. Walker; *Produced by* Hal Roach; *Cinematographer:* George Meehan; *Editor:* Richard Currier; *Cast:* Thelma Todd, ZaSu Pitts, Anita Garvin, Monte Collins, Bobby Burns, Otto Fries, Paulette Goddard, Charlie Hall, Lois January, Dorothy Vernon; *Released by* MGM on August 20, 1932; Two Reels

Thelma and ZaSu returned to Roach once production resumed after the annual break, with new contracts securing them continued work on their series of two-reel comedies. Despite her longing to do more varied roles, and the demands of the physical comedy, ZaSu appreciated the steady work and had become very good friends with Thelma. Thelma, who also longed to branch out, was realizing her talent for comedy was resulting in some of her most popular work.

Show Business is a particularly fascinating short, partly because it has the distinction of being the only Roach production directed by Jules White. White had done some comedy shorts at Educational Pictures for his brother Jack White, and now Jules and co-director Zion Meyers were at MGM doing a series called Dogville Comedies. In these very strange two-reelers, dogs are dressed up to parody current movies, with voices overdubbing their actions. Meyers and White also co-directed the 1931 Buster Keaton feature *Sidewalks of New York.*

Because he had some notoriety as a comedy director for MGM, which distributed the Roach product, Jules White found himself on the lot doing a Thelma Todd–ZaSu Pitts comedy. The results allow us to see White's very different style within the confines of the Roach methods. White would soon be hired to head the short subject department at Columbia studios, where he not only resurrected the fading careers of Harry Langdon and Buster Keaton, but continued the work of veterans Charley Chase and Andy Clyde. He is best known for his work with the Three Stooges, a trio whose violent slapstick style best represented White's comic vision. It is that vision that White brings, to some extent, here.

Show Business has Thelma and ZaSu living in a boarding house, waiting for the phone to ring to give their act, along with their pet monkey, a job performing on stage. They receive a call from a booking agency and must hurriedly board a train and be at the theater in an hour. There is a wild ride on the train, with several other acts also on board, and the girls' pet monkey getting away and causing havoc. The girls end up getting thrown off the train, never even arriving at their gig.

Show Business is filled with knockabout comedy in the Jules White tradition, with Thelma and ZaSu gamely performing their scenes in the roughneck manner as directed. The film first has them packing in such a hurry that ZaSu packs Thelma's only dress in the trunk which is then taken away. The resourceful Thelma throws a coat over her negligee and they head to the train station. At the station, the film introduces Anita Garvin as a haughty actress who compares herself to the likes of Ethel Barrymore and Gloria Swanson. The girls' pet monkey starts playing with Garvin's pampered dog. It also pulls her coat off the bench and tries to make a bed out of it. When the monkey starts climbing over the actress, she reacts big and it runs off. Thelma wanders past wearing a coat similar to the one owned by Garvin. She accuses Thelma of stealing from her and alerts a cop, who demands that Thelma remove the coat, which reveals negligee. The cop is shocked, reacts impulsively by removing his coat to cover Thelma, but this reveals that he isn't wearing a shirt.

These opening gags, while continuing the film's narrative, also reveal the more aggressive approach that Jules White employed. The anger that comes from each character is not the slow burn as employed by most Roach comics, but a more boisterous lashing out, with hollering and carrying on. Any subtlety comes from the actors. For instance, after a tug of war for the coat, Anita falls down and notices her own coat safely under the bench by her dog. Her reaction, a series of facial expressions, brilliantly conveys confusion, acceptance, embarrassment and a certain level of relief, all in a matter of seconds. Far better seen than described, it shows why Garvin was one of the most effective Roach players. According to film research archivist Richard Finegan, "Anita stated at a screening of this film later in her life that she really hated having that monkey climbing on her, and that her reactions of fear and disgust in the shots were genuine."

One fun bit on the train has a group of performers tricking Thelma and ZaSu by indicating that the drawing room is their quarters. It is actually the star's room, as shown in an establishing shot where Garvin is pleased to see the flowers and candy that await her. When Thelma and ZaSu enter the room, they naturally believe these surprises are for them—that is, of course, until they are reprimanded by the show's director and sent to an upper berth that they must somehow share.

Jules White notably used the same slapstick style whether he was working with women or men; for instance, at Columbia he used the same aggres-

Left to right: Anita Garvin, Otto Fries, ZaSu Pitts and Thelma Todd in *Show Business* (1932).

47

sive style for Vera Vague as he did for Andy Clyde. So when Thelma and ZaSu attempt to get into the upper berth, they climb over each other, become entangled, and fumble about in the rough manner that was far more Jules White than it was Hal Roach. Thelma and ZaSu have no trouble making it work, however, their expressions and maneuvers exhibiting their skill at physical comedy. Laurel and Hardy made an entire two-reeler out of being stuck in a train's cramped upper berth in their early talkie *Berth Marks* (1929).

Monte Collins, who often worked with Jules White throughout his career, plays the show supervisor who attempts to keep the egotistical actress happy. He's a bundle of frustrated anger as he insist the girls keep their monkey in the baggage car so that it doesn't upset Garvin. Collins' manner really isn't any less blustery than Roach stalwart Billy Gilbert, so his more aggressive manner fits in pretty well. The baggage car is locked, so the girls must conceal the monkey from the others. Of course it gets loose, ends up down Thelma's back, makes noises that ZaSu insists is due to her own bronchial trouble, and eventually gets the girls thrown off the train. However, in a neat twist, Garvin is ejected along with them!

A much more raucous comedy for Thelma and ZaSu, *Show Business* is an interesting look at how they respond to White's more forceful slapstick approach. While used the material again for the Three Stooges in their Columbia short *A Pain in the Pullman* (1936) and it works much better with them. In that film, the haughty actor is a male, played by James C. Morton (who appeared in several Roach comedies). The same story was again resurrected by White for the Columbia comedy *Training for Trouble* (1947) starring Gus Schilling and Richard Lane, with Monte Collins repeating his role as the harried manager, and even that film works better than *Show Business*. This is not to say that this Todd–Pitts short is a misfire. It just features material, and an approach, that didn't quite suit the girls as well as it would other comedians. *Variety* called *Show Business* "a better than average short—a builder-upper on any program"[16] and *Film Daily* proclaimed this comedy "a good one."[17] *Motion Picture Herald* was a bit more reserved, stating that *Show Business* was "reasonably amusing."[18]

About a week after this film was released, Thelma Todd was dining at the Brown Derby restaurant in Hollywood when a fire in the kitchen caused smoke to fill the entire building. Thelma and several other celebrities rushed out into the fresh air. Movie fans surrounded the area, and the police had to come in and restore order.

Before starting their next comedy, both Thelma Todd and ZaSu Pitts were, as usual, active in other projects. Todd played the title role in the independently produced feature *Klondike*, while ZaSu appeared in MGM's *Blondie of the Follies* and then was off to Universal for a supporting role in the film version of Fannie Hurst's novel *Back Street* with Irene Dunne. The duo was then back at the Roach studios to appear in one of their best comedies to date.

Alum and Eve (1932)

Directed by George Marshall; *Dialogue by* H.M. Walker; *Produced by* Hal Roach; *Cinematographer:* Hap Depew; *Editor:* Richard Currier; *Cast:* Thelma Todd, ZaSu Pitts, James C. Morton, Almeda Fowler, Betty Danko, Ham Kinsey, Bobby Burns, Otto Fries, Baldwin Cooke, Dorothy Layton; *Released by* MGM on September 24, 1932; Two Reels

Alum and Eve shows Thelma and ZaSu really maintaining their stride, and it emerges as another of the funniest of their comedies thus far. Although it is not as aggressive as Jules White's *Show Business*, there is plenty of rough slapstick and director George Marshall keeps things moving at a quick pace.

Hurrying to the beach, Thelma and ZaSu are stopped for speeding. Attempting to get out of the ticket, Thelma tells the officer that she is taking ZaSu to the hospital. He misunderstands, believing that ZaSu is pregnant. The girls must speed to the hospital, with the police providing an escort.

Thelma and ZaSu must go along with things until they can get away. But once at the hospital, a series of complications ensues. First, ZaSu is plopped into an open hamper instead of a bed, and gets caught. Thelma and the cop get entangled while trying to free her, as do some orderlies and nurses. It is one of those classic Hal Roach comedy situations where an initial situation builds to include others, and it offers some good roughhouse slapstick as they all twist and turn in an attempt to free themselves.

Several nurses, each holding a baby, come out of a room, and the officer reacts amusingly, believing each baby has come from ZaSu. The confused officer is especially incredulous when the final nurse comes out with an entire slew of newborns. It is a nice gag sequence and James C. Morton uses his veteran comic skills quite effectively, offering some good reactions.

The cop is distracted by Thelma while ZaSu is taken away by orderlies and nurses who try to undress her as she fights back. More roughhouse slapstick ensues as two nurses struggle with ZaSu. Thelma comes to her rescue and ZaSu complains, "They want to take out my other appendix." After the cop gets suspicious, the girls change their story from pregnancy to a dog bite, and they are taken into an examination room. As they burst through the door, some alum is knocked into a pitcher of water, and everyone who drinks from that pitcher starts puckering up. The girls attempt to escape out a window, but as she climbs out, Thelma's dress gets caught and is torn off her body. The cop comes along and tries to pull ZaSu back in through the window, but she ends up pulling him out.

At this point, we are at about the midway point of the two-reeler and it has already established its premise, presented its conflict, and has continued to build gags upon the situation. This has now become the formula for a Thelma Todd–ZaSu Pitts two-reeler. It had been established in earlier movies, but in *Alum and Eve* it appears to culminate as something that has been honed to perfection. After some tentativeness in the earliest films, and a few experiments along the way, in this, their eleventh film, they seem comfortable with their roles and the formula of their comedies. When they secured Gus Meins as a consistent director of their films, the series' formula would be further refined.

It is quite funny how such a small thing—Thelma and ZaSu telling a white lie to get out of trouble with the cop—spirals out of control to the point where an entire hospital is thrown into chaos. And while director Marshall creates a film that is fast-paced, there is still a definite progression of escalating situations. There are a couple gags we've seen in previous films—like a reluctant ZaSu being forced to undress—but they seem to work more effectively in this film.

Again, as these are pre–Code movies with women doing physical comedy, there are sequences that would have been considered risqué at the time. Thelma losing her clothing as she climbs out the window, the nurses wrestling ZaSu on the bed causing their uniforms to open at the front which exposes their undergarments, and the close struggles involving both men and women, are all pretty edgy for the early 1930s. There is really no holding back with the physical comedy here. It may seem a bit awkward in the more enlightened 21st century, but hilariously so.

As the scantily clad Thelma climbs in another window in another part of the hospital, the scene cuts to a patient with large casts on each leg, being told he'll never walk again. When the half-dressed Thelma climbs into his window and runs through his room, the incapacitated patient immediately gets up and starts chasing her. There's a lot of chasing, narrow escapes and

ZaSu and Thelma in their car while James C. Morton watches from around the corner in *Alum and Eve* (1932).

captures before both Thelma and ZaSu are finally caught and carried into a hospital room. Meanwhile, the cop drinks the alum, is thought to be foaming at the mouth, and is accosted by the doctors and nurses. Thelma and ZaSu get hold of some ether and escape down the hall in slow motion as the picture fades.

Motion Picture Herald (August 13, 1932) called the film "fast moving" and stated "[T]here's more laugh-provoking action than usual."[19] *Film Daily* (February 16, 1933) called it "a good comedy that has plenty of laughs" and "lots of amusing slapstick action."[20] It is a comedy that never lets up, containing scene after scene of wild slapstick gags. Everything seems to work. Perhaps some might find the roughhousing off-putting, especially seeing men and women tangled together and struggling to free themselves, but within the context of this two-reeler it comes off as absurdly amusing.

The supporting cast of familiar Roach stalwarts is good, but character actor James C. Morton is especially funny as the cop, playing off of Thelma and ZaSu in a manner that spotlights himself while still enhancing the starring comedy team. This sort of balance takes a great deal of talent, and Morton effectively pulls it off. He would appear often in Roach films and later in several Columbia comedies before his death in 1942.

Now that the formula for a Todd–Pitts comedy had been honed, and the women were settled completely into their roles and their on-screen relationship, their shorts were more consistent and amusing. Thelma made no other movie appearances before her next short comedy with ZaSu. Ms. Pitts appeared in two feature films. She was top-billed, over second-billed James Gleason in the indie mystery comedy *The Crooked Circle* for low-budget producer E.W Hammons, and then took a smaller supporting role in the Universal release *Once in a Lifetime*, which starred Jack Oakie.

The Soilers (1932)

Directed by George Marshall; *Dialogue by* H.M. Walker; *Produced by* Hal Roach; *Cinematographer:* Hap Depew; *Editor:* Richard Currier; *Cast:* Thelma Todd, ZaSu Pitts, James C. Morton, Bud Jamison, Ernie Alexander, Charlie Hall, Sam Lufkin, George Marshall, William J. O'Brien; *Released by* MGM on October 29, 1932; Two Reels

ZaSu Pitts continued to be distracted by opportunities outside of the Hal Roach comedies in which she was appearing with Thelma Todd. But she continued to re-sign for more comedies, despite some misgivings, due to the steady work. Another reason was that Hal Roach continued to give both actresses the freedom to seek work elsewhere. A blurb in the September 13, 1932, *Film Daily* stated, "Thelma Todd and ZaSu Pitts will begin their next Hal Roach comedy within a few weeks. In between the comedy series, the latest of which is *The Soilers*, they are given a roving commission by the studio to appear in pictures for other producers."[21]

Some have opined that the Roach publicity people put that story in the trades to emphasize the fact that both actresses had that freedom to work outside of their comedy shorts series. Renewal time was soon approaching and the studio did not want to lose one of its more popular comedy teams, dubbed in some reviews as "the female Laurel and Hardy," which is lofty praise indeed.

Prior to filming *The Soilers*, Thelma Todd married Pat De Cicco, who has been described as a small-time mobster. He became a controversial figure in Thelma's life. The marriage was difficult from the start. So, between ZaSu

Shooting a scene with Pitts and Todd for *The Soilers* (1932).

being distracted by her interest in extending her range as an actress, and Thelma's being distracted by her personal life, it is impressive that *The Soilers* comes off as one of the duo's better comedies.

The Soilers, the duo's twelfth film, pretty carefully responds to the formula that Todd and Pitts had established. Opening with the girls as unsuccessful door-to-door magazine subscription sellers, it curiously starts out showing ZaSu, alone, trying to make a sale but getting a door slammed in her face. She exhibits energy and charm, but when the door slams she slips back into her forlorn persona. Thelma then approaches, and the two commiserate as to their lack of success.

This opening is curious because it would stand to reason that Thelma would be the aggressive go-getter who used her charms to sell magazines while ZaSu offered support. Instead the film presents a different dynamic, spotlighting ZaSu but not showing what Thelma might have done differently in an effort to make a sale. In any case, neither of the girls was successful. They concoct an idea to go downtown and try selling the magazines to men, believing their charm might be more effective in that setting.

53

The first slapstick mishap happens soon afterward. ZaSu is eating a banana, about the only sustenance the girls can afford, and a man (Bud Jamison) walks by and slips on the discarded peel. Immediately the girls approach him on the ground and give him their spiel for selling magazines, in unison. He barks at them to go away, but they end up stumbling over him, landing on top of him, and becoming entangled. A man (James C. Morton) comes out of his nearby house, tries to help and ends up tangled with them. It is this type of sequence that only works in pre–Code films. Two women in dresses tangled together within the bodies of two men has a risqué quality even in the 21st century. It is established that Morton is a judge and Jamison his newly hired bodyguard.

This sequence is almost immediately followed by a revolving door gag where the girls attempt to enter an office building but keep getting caught within it. The door picks up some velocity and shoots ZaSu into a custodian holding a ladder and a bucket of soap and water. The ladder starts spinning, causing the water to spill. Thelma then gets involved, as so Jamison and Morton. One of the film's highlights, it is a classic Roach sight gag that builds nicely.

Slapstick gags seem to be more predominant in *The Soilers* than the previous Todd–Pitts comedies except perhaps the exceptionally aggressive *Show Business*. For instance, ZaSu discards another banana peel, Jamison slips on it again, and when he angrily barks at a diminutive elevator operator (Charlie Hall), the elevator man walks out and punches the much larger Jamison, knocking him down, then returns to his elevator. It is carefully and precisely timed, and, although only seconds long, is another comic highlight.

Entangled situations seem to be a running gag. When the girls attempt to sell their wares to Morton in his office, the entanglements get so involved that the three are soon covered in glue and ink. The girls later get involved with jurors in Morton's courtroom, and get the entire jury entangled. This allows them to find and get rid of a bomb that two anarchists planted in the courtroom.

The entangled situations made up the bulk of the gags, and with the funniest one coming early in the film. The premise of *The Soilers* isn't too far off from the previous film *Alum and Eve*, but it's approached differently. In the previous film, Thelma and ZaSu accidentally end up in the hospital and wreak havoc trying to get out. In this film, they are in the office building on a mission, and cause chaos through their bumbling.

The Soilers is a perfectly outrageous two-reeler filled with slapstick and risqué situations, messiness, violence, pratfalls, entangled bodies and a climactic explosion. It is wildly funny and one of the Todd–Pitts shorts that holds up best. It also explores the relationship between Thelma and ZaSu more carefully. There is a scene where the two are in an office trying to make a sale. Thelma is carefully using her feminine attributes to attract the man, and subtly interesting him as she demonstrates a machine that rolls cigarettes. ZaSu continually interrupts in her attempts to help, throwing off the pace and disrupting Thelma's gradual success with the man. It is funny, but also quite fascinating in showing an inherent conflict within the duo's relationship. Thelma is in charge, in control, understands the situation. ZaSu believes she is, but her attempts to be supportive are actually a distraction. Thelma fumes and tries to signal to ZaSu to back off, but ZaSu doesn't understand. This has some similarities to the Laurel and Hardy dynamic, but played from the perspective of the two actresses. Their approach is a successful one and helps further define the team.

The supporting cast once again helps make the film that much more effective, with performers that the duo had worked with in other films, includ-

ZaSu Pitts and Thelma Todd in *The Soilers* (1932).

ing the aforementioned Jamison, Morton and Hall. Director George Marshall can be spotted doing a bit as a helpful bystander.

Upon completion of *The Soilers*, Thelma went to Columbia to play the female lead in Lewis Seiler's *Deception*, about corruption in the pro wrestling business. She then co-starred in her friend Clara Bow's penultimate film *Call Her Savage* at Fox. Bow and Todd have the same birthday (Bow is one year older). ZaSu was also busy, appearing at Paramount in Harry Joe Brown's feature *Madison Square Garden* that included some shots filmed on location at the famous arena.

Sneak Easily (1932)

Directed by Gus Meins; *Produced by* Hal Roach; *Cinematographer:* Art Lloyd; *Editor:* Richard Currier; *Cast:* Thelma Todd, ZaSu Pitts, Billy Gilbert, James C. Morton, Bobby Burns, Rolfe Sedan, Charlie Hall, Harry Bernard, Billy Bletcher (voice only); *Released by* MGM on December 10, 1932; Two Reels

Gravely ill, Thelma Todd was hospitalized just prior to filming *Sneak Easily*. The official story was that she had developed peritonitis from an abscess, but Hal Roach would later state that it was likely a miscarriage or maybe even an abortion. According to Michelle Morgan's book *The Ice Cream Blonde*, Thelma was well enough to attend the funeral of her friend Belle Bennett on November 6.[22] She began shooting *Sneak Easily* on November 9.

Perhaps because of her recent hospitalization, Thelma has less to do in *Sneak Easily*. It is really ZaSu's film with Thelma in support. The story has Thelma playing a defense attorney trying to prove that an oddball scientist did not kill his wife by substituting an explosive pill for a diet pill. A dummy device and the actual explosive are exhibits. When the bailiff brings them out, the identification cards get mixed up. Thelma indicates that no woman could swallow something so big, holding up the large black object. Juror ZaSu insists she can, and tries. Meanwhile, the explosive rolls off a table and falls to the floor. When it does not explode, everyone realizes that was the dummy and that ZaSu swallowed the explosive.

The comedy here is all reactive. First, Thelma cannot let the others know that one of the jurors is her best friend and roommate. So she angrily glares at ZaSu when the latter says things like, "Did you remember to turn the gas off under the roast?" But most of the reactive comedy occurs once the bomb and dummy bomb are introduced. The film is gradually paced until the supposed explosive starts rolling along the table and about to hit the floor. Suddenly, people scream and run for cover. One person jumps out of their shoes and runs off. Defense attorney Billy Gilbert tries to hide under the robe of judge James C. Morton. Thelma jumps over the judge's bench and topples to the floor with him. All we see are their legs tangled together in what appears to hide a risqué position.

The remainder of the film has the others reacting to ZaSu having swallowed the explosive. They have ten minutes to get to the scientist's lab, where he can create an antidote. The lab is eight minutes away. Director Gus Meins beautifully frames a shot where everyone in the courtroom is slowly escorting ZaSu outside and into a waiting ambulance. With every stumble, the entire crowd surrounding her reacts. Once in the ambulance, more varying forms of comic tension are introduced, from the vehicle racing across bumpy roads to ZaSu having the hiccups. Once they arrive at the laboratory, the professor hurries to concoct an antidote, when his wife shows up. Seeing

Left to right: Bobby Burns, Thelma Todd, James C. Morton, ZaSu Pitts, Billy Gilbert in *Sneak Easily* (1932).

that she is alive and well, it is realized that what ZaSu swallowed is completely harmless.

Meins, working on his first Todd–Pitts short, was one of the more creative Roach Studio directors. He began in the 1920s directing the Buster Brown comedies, a kids' series that likely prepared him for his subsequent work on Roach's Our Gang comedies. Meins directed most of the ensuing films in the Todd–Pitts series over the next several years, and offered a new creative dimension. While a formula was already becoming established, it was Meins who refined it. And although there had been, and would be, several different directors who effectively handled the actresses and their material, it isn't too much of a stretch to claim that Meins likely made the most significant contribution.

For *Sneak Easily*, Meins created a neat opening where a shot of a cop on the phone irises into a larger picture of police cars headed to the destination. Meins shoots the courtroom footage with an expanse that keeps the action in the frame, cutting to medium shots as Thelma and prosecuting attorney Billy Gilbert make their respective cases. When blustery Gilbert addresses the jury, Meins shoots him in close-up. And while the ambulance ride is shot in front of a process screen, Meins cuts away to actual road footage quickly enough so the fakery of the process does not register.

This sort of learned filmmaking brought a lot to this comedy, and to subsequent Meins comedies. He later became exclusive to the Our Gang series, as he seemed to work best with them, but not before he made a strong impact on the films of Thelma Todd and ZaSu Pitts.

Bobby Burns offers an amusingly eccentric turn as the scientist. His fiendish look in most cases is changed to one of delight when he sees the bomb rolling off the table and about to go off. He is reduced to cowering when his heavyset wife confronts him in the lab. When the judge asks her, "You didn't blow up?" she responds, "No, this is my normal weight!"

While *Sneak Easily* is very funny, and at the time was one of the most popular Todd–Pitts shorts, the lack of team dynamic makes it less effective than *The Soilers* or *Alum and Eve*. Spotlighting ZaSu, with Thelma in support, gave Pitts the opportunity to do more with her character, and that likely pleased the actress and her interest in branching out.

It was an interesting choice to have Thelma play an attorney. Her character could just as easily have been a fellow juror and she could have acted more on equal footing with ZaSu. This film is definitely a lot less wild than the last two, with the supporting players engaging in most of the slapstick within their reactions to ZaSu, instead of the duo taking part in the physical comedy themselves.

Thelma and ZaSu began shooting their next two-reel comedy *Asleep in the Feet* only 12 days after completing *Sneak Easily*. Thus, there was no time between two-reelers to work in movies at other studios. However, Thelma's Columbia film *Air Hostess* was released around the same time as *Sneak Easily*, and so was a comedy feature ZaSu did with Slim Summerville at Universal, *They Just Had to Get Married*. Although ZaSu's comedies with Summerville were B movies, they had more prestige in the industry than short subjects.

There were only a few shorts left before the women would again be negotiating their contracts with Hal Roach. While each of them had aspirations to explore other activities at other studios, and each wanted to offer some creative contributions to their comedies together, Thelma was basically satisfied with the work they were doing at Roach, and ZaSu wanted to move away from slapstick short comedies.

Asleep in the Feet (1933)

Directed by Gus Meins; *Produced by* Hal Roach; *Cinematographer:* Art Lloyd; *Editor:* Richard Currier; *Cast:* Thelma Todd, ZaSu Pitts, Billy Gilbert, Eddie Dunn, Anita Garvin, Kay Lavelle, Nora Cecil, Julia Griffith, Nelson McDowell, Tiny Ward, Lew Davis, Jack Hill, Ham Kinsey, Charles Dorety, Betty Danko, Ruth Adams; *Released by* MGM on January 21, 1933; Two Reels

Asleep in the Feet is one of the funniest two-reelers in the Thelma Todd–ZaSu Pitts series. It features amusing situations, good slapstick, it examines the girls' relationship, and it benefits from Gus Meins' skillful direction.

Department store workers Thelma and ZaSu share a room in a boarding house. They overhear that a fellow tenant will be thrown out if she doesn't come up with $20 toward her rent. They ask Anita Garvin, another boarder, who works as a taxi dancer, if she has the money to lend them so they can lend it to her. As taxi dancers only get ten cents a dance, she thanks them for the compliment, but states that they might be able to drum up some money by becoming dancers themselves.

The girls go to the dance hall where Thelma has many interested, but her time is occupied by burly sailor Eddie Dunn. ZaSu contends with a man whose pointy beard tickles her face, and another who is large and bumbling. When ZaSu's shoe loses a heel, she and Thelma go into a dressing room to repair it. While there, Anita tells them they can generate more money if they flirt a bit more with their dancers.

Two haughty women and a pretentious officer enter the hall to check out the goings-on. Manager Billy Gilbert gathers the dancers and asks them to "dance like their grandmothers" and instructs the band to play a light waltz, so the inspectors believe the place is staid and conservative. Just then ZaSu comes out of the dressing room, having been heavily made up by Anita, and starts suggestively gyrating about the dance floor, soon joined by the officer who is "investigating."

The film concludes with the officer discovering the burly sailor is his nephew. As the two embrace, Thelma and ZaSu get away. Still nowhere near the $20 they need, the girls see another woman complaining about having received a black eye from another, and demands a $20 payment from the manager to keep quiet. Just then, the lights go out, and when they come on, Thelma has a black eye. They also get $20. When they get home, Thelma examines her eye in the mirror and sees an indentation that matches ZaSu's ring, revealing that it is she who punched her. ZaSu starts to cry and says, "Well, at least we got the $20!" Thelma just bursts out laughing.

The film starts with good visual ideas. Cooking in their room against the house rules, the girls hide a hot plate under a phonograph lid. When they are interrupted by a knock at the door from the landlady, they must quickly hide the fact that they are cooking. The slapstick conclusion of this portion of the short has the stew toppling out the window and onto the landlady's head below.

The film picks up its rhythm when Thelma and ZaSu are at the dance hall. Director Gus Meins' ability to frame the action is especially evident when shooting the dancers, the various areas of action each complimenting each other in the long shots and medium shots. Close-ups are used when ZaSu is dancing with the large, bumbling gentleman and the heel comes off her shoe. He steps into the errant heel and starts dancing lopsidedly. It is all worked out nicely, with Meins cutting from the floor, to the faces, and then to medium shots containing both areas in the frame. It is very funny, and very effectively filmed. In their previous films, the girls engaged in very rough slapstick that could just as well have been done by a man. Here, the physical comedy of losing the heel is centered around problems that only a woman would likely have.

The direction is even more impressive when the manager gathers the dancers and has them dance "like their grandmothers" while the band plays

Left to right: Thelma Todd, Billy Gilbert, ZaSu Pitts and Ham Kinsey in *Asleep in the Feet* (1933).

a waltz, for the benefit of the visiting police. Meins shoots the dance floor in a medium shot, and when ZaSu goes out and starts to shimmy about, her movements offset the staid waltzers who occupy the negative space. It is really quite remarkable, and once again shows Meins' keen directorial vision.

The relationship of Thelma and ZaSu is examined nicely in virtually every scene. It is again reinforced that Thelma is the sexy, desirable one and ZaSu is the ugly ducking wallflower. Thelma does a wonderfully funny double-take upon first seeing a made-up ZaSu. And, when ZaSu is on the dance floor with the policeman and suggests they try one of the steps she sees another doing, the two of them tumble to the floor. Meins cuts back to Thelma, reacting to the situation. It is this sort of cause-and-effect, execution-and-response that gives comic depth to the duo's relationship.

However, the most significant presentation of the duo's relationship comes when ZaSu douses the lights and hits Thelma, sacrificing her friend for the good of one even less fortunate. Thelma is too proud of her meek comrade to be angry. The concluding shot of a weeping ZaSu and a laughing Thelma is one of the best endings in the series. The warmth between the two ladies seems very genuine.

Asleep in the Feet is something of a cultural artifact with a certain historical significance. The concept of taxi dancers receiving ten cents per dance is a bit of popular culture from America's past. It began in dance academies, but soon spread to dance halls and peaked in the 1920s. By the time this film was made in the early 1930s, it was presented as a way for women to pick up a bit of extra money during the Great Depression.

Asleep in the Feet was very popular, according to distributor reports in the trades. *Hollywood Filmograph* suggested in an article that Thelma, ZaSu, Billy Gilbert and Eddie Dunn were "drawing in the laughs" and praised Meins' direction.[23] They stated, "We would like to see this combination followed out by Hal Roach as to the stars and the director, for the film looks like everyone was happy when it was made." They also added that a sneak preview audience "enjoyed many a hearty laugh… [*Asleep in the Feet*] will be one of their funniest funfests."

Asleep in the Feet is great fun and spotlights the work of both Thelma Todd and ZaSu Pitts effectively. There were only three films left on their Roach contract, so the producer filmed them in rapid succession.

Maids a la Mode (1933)

Directed by Gus Meins; *Produced by* Hal Roach; *Cinematographer:* Hap Depew; *Editor:* Louis McManus; *Cast:* Thelma Todd, ZaSu Pitts, Billy Gilbert, Cissy Fitzgerald, Harry Bernard, Kay Deslys, Charlie Hall, Marvin Hatley, Sydney Jarvis, Mary Kornman, John J. Richardson, Leo White; *Released by* MGM on March 4, 1933; Two Reels

Hal Roach was aware of ZaSu Pitts' lessened interest in doing the two-reelers and wanted to get as many produced as possible before her contract was up. He understood that she was a dedicated performer who would do her best in each of the films, even without opportunity to work elsewhere between productions.

Thelma Todd had her own problems. On January 22, 1933, she and husband Pat De Cicco were involved in a car accident. The actress suffered a broken shoulder, cracked ribs and other injuries. She had the strength to recover quickly, and went back to work on the Roach comedies.

Maids a la Mode maintains the established Todd–Pitts comedy formula, and also follows the structure of situational humor laced with slapstick. ZaSu is a seamstress and Thelma is a model for dress designer Billy Gilbert. They are assigned to deliver some expensive dresses, but en route they are stopped by a former employer of Thelma's who invites them to a swanky party and won't take no for an answer. They decide to wear the dresses they were assigned to deliver. After a series of slapstick complications, the girls are shocked to see Billy Gilbert arrive and react angrily to their wearing the dresses they were supposed to deliver. They make a hasty exit.

The opening of *Maids a la Mode* establishes the characters, as well as both ZaSu and Thelma's roles. ZaSu's bumbling seamstress gets in the way of Thelma attempting to model the designer's new fashions, causing a ruckus that results in a moving runway that is out of control, and the designer falling onto ZaSu's pincushion, filled with pins. It is all a lot of typical roughhouse slapstick that helps to establish the situation on which the film's structure can build.

One fascinating thing about older films is how they offer a peek into another era. The models walking on a conveyor belt is something they did then and not now. It provides a good opportunity for humor. Further amusement is provided by the haughty, wealthy woman for whom the girls are modeling, and her meek fiancé, who is suddenly very interested in the fashion show once the girls start modeling lingerie.

There is more slapstick on the street, after the girls are on their way to deliver the dresses and have been invited to the party. ZaSu steps onto a mattress left out for the junk man, pulls out a spring and gets it tangled onto another man. This bit of slapstick is tangential to what's going on in the film. It's funny, but appears to be a bit in the way.

The most inspired physical comedy occurs at the party. The women are wearing the dresses they were supposed to deliver, but it is discovered that ZaSu has some long underwear beneath hers. A drunk sees a loose string behind her and starts to pull, as an unwitting ZaSu walks away. When he finally comes to the end, he has removed the underwear beneath her dress, and the open back reveals a bit too much. Thelma notices this on the dance floor and keeps trying to reach up and lift the back of ZaSu's dress to cover her better, but manages only to pull a drunk's shirt tail out of his pants.

Thelma decides to remedy things by having ZaSu stand against some drapes, while Thelma attempts to sew up the back of the dress from the other side. Just then, Billy Gilbert arrives at the party. When the girls attempt to run away, it is discovered that Thelma has sewn ZaSu to the drapes. She starts swinging and knocking things down, grabbing a large mask and putting it over Gilbert's head. When she runs away, Thelma grabs the back of the drapes and is pulled along the slippery floor on a rug in a neat concluding visual.

Once again director Gus Meins exhibits a keen visual sense in both the slapstick scenes and those that concentrate on narrative exposition. Meins quickly impressed the Roach producers with his shot composition in the shorts he directed. Most of his work was with Our Gang, but when he'd helm a Todd–Pitts short, he knew how to frame the raucous scenes so that all of the action was effectively in the shot. This is especially impressive during the dance scene. Thelma and ZaSu each have dance partners and comically move about the floor among the other dancers. Meins follows the action so that we can see Thelma reaching, as she passes, for the back of ZaSu's dress in order to pull it up and conceal her bare back. The timing is very tight as Thelma inadvertently pulls the drunk's shirt tail out. This happens twice and all of it is done as everyone, except the drunk, is moving. The whole thing is blocked with precision and is one of the more impressive scenes in the comedy.

Maids a la Mode has a fun supporting cast, with Billy Gilbert typically standing out with his boisterous performance. The man who insists on Thelma and ZaSu attending the party is played by a flamboyant Leo White, who kisses each woman's hand vigorously, pinches their cheeks, and plays up his part with real gusto. White had a pretty extensive career in silent films, including several featuring Charlie Chaplin. In fact, when Chaplin left the Essanay studios, White was assigned by the studio heads to extend the comedian's two-reel *Burlesque on Carmen* (1916) to nearly four reels. For years, it was the four-reel cut that was available, and it appeared to be a confusing mess. More recently, Chaplin's original two-reel cut was restored, and the film's original aesthetic was greatly improved. Apparently, however, Chaplin held no grudge against White, using him in his later films like *The Great Dictator* (1940). White had quite an extensive career, appearing in films with

Harold Lloyd, Ben Turpin, W.C. Fields and the Three Stooges. He was also seen in the silent classics *Blood and Sand, Ben-Hur* and *Sunrise.*

The response to White's character offers some of the best comedy. When he is in the studio inviting Billy Gilbert to his party, he hugs and kisses him like an affectionate lap dog, until Gilbert agrees, just to get him to stop. When he vigorously kisses the hands of Thelma and ZaSu, their reaction is also quite amusing. Thelma fumes, but reacts less than the nonplussed ZaSu because she knows him.

The comedy of ZaSu and Thelma was now working like a well-oiled machine. ZaSu comfortably lapses into character, while Thelma's sarcasm and double-takes play off perfectly. The actresses seem to understand each another as performers. It is unfortunate that Pitts continued to find work on the Roach comedies to be more strenuous than she liked. While she played the physical comedy without incident, always turning in a fun performance, her heart was not in it. Since she and Thelma were off-screen friends, she confided in her that when their contracts were up, she was going to try to negotiate for more money and better conditions.

The Bargain of the Century (1933)

Directed by Charley Chase; *Produced by* Hal Roach; *Cinematographer:* Art Lloyd; *Editor:* Jack Ogilvie; *Cast:* Thelma Todd, ZaSu Pitts, Billy Gilbert, James P. Burtis, Frank Alexander, Harry Bernard, Fay Holderness, May Wallace; *Released by* MGM on April 8, 1933; Two Reels

The fact that Charley Chase directed *The Bargain of the Century* makes it stand out as significant. Chase was one of the top actors and directors at Roach, and had been since joining the company in 1924. He started his career a good ten years earlier, having worked for Mack Sennett's Keystone studio in films featuring Charlie Chaplin, the Keystone Cops and others. He started directing early on, learning the rudiments of the filmmaking process as cinema itself was growing. He continued to direct, and act, until his death in 1940. Chase was quite fond of Thelma Todd, having worked with her in several of his own films prior to Roach teaming her with ZaSu Pitts. As stated earlier in the text, Chase was quite interested in teaming with Thelma himself, but Roach wanted Thelma in her own series rather than adding her to an existing one that was already successful.

With Chase at the helm, *The Bargain of the Century* emerges as perhaps the funniest of the Thelma Todd–ZaSu Pitts films. For the first portion of the film, Chase takes part of the idea from his 1927 silent comedy *Fluttering Hearts* and revamps it for Thelma and ZaSu. He then creates a situation from that premise and builds upon it. The usual formula for a Todd–Pitts short is utilized in a different manner, and it is most effective.

Chase directed only two Roach films that were not his own starring vehicles, this one and *Music in Your Ears* (1934) with Billy Gilbert. Gilbert has the same character name in the later film as he does here, but he does not play the same character. It was likely Chase's friendship with Gilbert that resulted in his agreeing to helm an experimental film with Billy as the star. It didn't quite work out, but Gilbert later starred in a series called the Taxi Boys that had the unfortunate distinction of being one of the least interesting short comedy series produced by Roach during the sound era.

The Bargain of the Century has Thelma and ZaSu speeding to a department store sale, evading Officer Butterworth, the motorcycle cop who is chasing them. They are finally caught once they park just outside the store, but to get out of a ticket, they tell the cop that ZaSu is the daughter of his boss the lieutenant. Impressed, the cop agrees to help them brave the crowded, tumultuous department store sale. In the midst of this, they all get their clothing torn up. As they leave the store, they run into the lieutenant. Seeing Butterworth out of uniform, and insulted that the cop thought a "palooka" like ZaSu was his daughter, the lieutenant fires the officer. Feeling sorry for him, the girls hire Butterworth as a housekeeper and cook. Tiring of his intrusive presence after a couple of weeks, they invite the lieutenant's boss, the police chief, to dinner in order to make amends. Things do not go quite as planned. But, fortunately, they end with the cop getting back his job. Thelma is glad to be rid of him when ZaSu drops the bombshell that she and the cop are now engaged!

Chase's direction is impressive right from the opening scene. He starts the film with a speeding auto knocking down a traffic cop, which causes an officer on a motorcycle to chase them. The car runs through puddles which splash back at the pursuing cop. Unlike many Roach productions from around this time, this scene does not rely on rear projection that have caused other films to date badly. Chase uses mostly location footage in the long shots, while the close-ups of the cop being splashed with water are too quick for their back projection fakery to register. Chase films the cop being splashed, then cuts away to actual road footage. It makes the opening that much funnier and more effective.

Once the cop, Thelma and ZaSu enter the crowded store where a large group of women surround the bed sheets on sale, Chase draws from his silent *Fluttering Hearts* for a gag where the cop gets closer to the merchandise by tickling women to get them out of the way. When he inadvertently tickles Thelma, she turns around and punches him. ZaSu isn't faring any better: A heavyset man gives her his phone number and instructs her, "Ask for Elmer."

The scenes in the apartment include more good laughs. Butterworth has filled the home with booby traps, including a boxing glove on a spring release

Thelma Todd and ZaSu Pitts flank director Charley Chase (*Bargain of the Century* [1933]).

that activates upon opening the kitchen door, and a blaring siren that goes off when the apartment door opens. Out in the street, ZaSu slips on a banana peel that had been thrown there by the police chief. He offers to carry her up to her apartment, and there he meets Thelma and Butterworth, who has never met the chief of police. The girls try to use the opportunity to impress the chief and get Butterworth his job back.

Butterworth grabs the chief's watch to perform a magic trick, and ends up destroying it. Remnants of the destroyed watch end up in the homemade ice cream they're eating, so every time the chief spoons up a glob of the dessert and reveals part of the watch, Thelma or Butterworth throw more ice cream in his dish to cover it up. This becomes a rather rhythmic gag situation. The chief spoons some ice cream, Thelma puts more in his bowl, he turns to her and insists he wants no more, and Butterworth plops some in. It is a wonderfully performed back-and-forth visual that is expertly timed, and punctuated by the chief's pleas for "no more ice cream!" Chase frames it in a medium shot with occasional cutaways to a close-up of the chief. Billy Gilbert plays the chief with all of his delightful bluster.

When the chief gets up to leave, he opens the apartment door and activates the siren. He reacts in a frightened manner and runs toward the kitchen, being hit by the boxing glove that springs out and knocks him unconscious. The police, alerted to the siren, enter the apartment and arrest the chief, who is an imposter. Butterworth gets the credit and is put back on the force. Thelma, reacting to ZaSu's announcement that she and Butterworth are engaged, opens the kitchen door so the boxing glove hits ZaSu.

Chase's inspired direction is the main reason why *The Bargain of the Century* stands out as the best of the Thelma–ZaSu films. Chase creates a more comfortable dynamic between the two women. This comedy does not spotlight ZaSu nor does it single out Thelma. In fact, the duo works more cohesively as a team in this film than any of their previous ones. They respond to situations and engage in slapstick, and each gets plenty of opportunities to be funny. ZaSu's attempts to flirt and Thelma's wide-eyed double takes are still utilized as part of the formula, but neither appears to be given more attention than the other.

James Burtis appeared in only a few Roach productions, usually in very small parts. His performance here as Butterworth is one of his larger roles and he does nicely. Burtis made a career out of playing small roles, appearing in over 100 movies. The heavyset man who gives ZaSu his number in one of the film's funnier moments is Frank "Fatty" Alexander, who appeared often

3. The Films of Thelma Todd and ZaSu Pitts

in Larry Semon silents and was part of the Ton of Fun Trio with Fat Karr and Kewpie Ross.

The Bargain of the Century turned out to be the most popular of the duo's comedies, securing greater bookings based on exhibitor reports that audiences thoroughly enjoyed the film.

One Track Minds (1933)

Directed by Gus Meins; *Produced by* Hal Roach; *Cinematographer:* Hap Depew; *Editor:* Louis McManus; *Cast:* Thelma Todd, ZaSu Pitts, George "Spanky" McFarland, Billy Gilbert, Lucien Prival, Jack Clifford, Sterling Holloway, Billy Bletcher, Charlie Hall, Eddie Tamblyn, Baldwin Cooke, Helen Dale; *Released by* MGM on May 20, 1933; Two Reels

One Track Minds was the last Thelma Todd–ZaSu Pitts comedy in their current contract. Neither Thelma nor ZaSu realized this would be their last two-reel comedy together, even though Todd already signed for eight more films and ZaSu had not done so.

Back as director, Gus Meins opens the film nicely with shots of a moving train beneath the credits. Thelma and ZaSu are traveling with Spanky, a boy whose mischief is quite a distraction as the girls travel to Roaring Lion Studios where Thelma, a hometown beauty contest winner, is headed to enter movies. The director to whom she is to report, the haughty and demanding Von Sternheim, enters the train area along with his toadying assistant. The director insists on sitting where Thelma and ZaSu are, believing it is the best vantage point. Not knowing who he is, they refuse.

A lot of elements are offered here. First, the director's flamboyance and the girls' reaction to him. Then the reaction to the harried conductor Billy Gilbert, each of them using affected German accents. The various conflicts are established before director Meins offers his first big slapstick scene: The train vendor is an old friend of the girls' from the laundry where they once all worked. He gives Spanky a toy airplane and offers ZaSu some caramels and Thelma some nuts (with the comment "Nuts to you!"). ZaSu tries to help Spanky fly his toy plane, losing control and causing it to fly through the train car. It knocks off a man's toupee, stabs a man in the beard, and also infiltrates the director's seat. It is a quick bit of visual comedy that disrupts the action, while setting up the subsequent sequences.

A hard-of-hearing man tries to converse with ZaSu, misinterpreting everything she says. When he shows her his prize bees, ZaSu asks, "Don't they sting?" whereupon he replies, "No, not a note!" The director becomes upset with the loud voices and reacts angrily, only to be admonished by Thelma sticking up for her friend. After they notice a newspaper identifying Von Sternheim, Thelma goes to freshen up so she looks her best. Returning to her seat, she starts coyly smiling and waving at the director, and then starts a recitation hoping he will notice her. An opportunity arises when they overhear that the director's leading lady has walked off his latest production. He gives Thelma a script to work from as a makeshift audition. ZaSu attempts to read lines with her, but keeps fouling things up.

The conclusion has the bee container getting knocked over, causing the bees to fly about the train and start stinging everyone in a neat visual effect that causes good tumultuous laughs. Thelma, ZaSu and Spanky hide in a laundry basket as the film abruptly comes to an end.

Thelma Todd, cinematographer Hap Depew and ZaSu Pitts look at strips of film on the set of *One Track Minds* (1933).

There are funny moments in *One Track Minds*, but they seem randomly placed rather than effectively structured. The idea of limiting the setting to the train car is an interesting concept, but little is made of the cramped quarters, disparate personalities and opportunities for things to go wrong. Many of the gags become loose ends in and of themselves. ZaSu drinks a glass of liquid soap, believing it to be water, and starts blowing bubbles, but in the next scene she is okay. And while the bees flying about the train car is a fun visual, it appears to be a handy way to end the film with a big gag without concluding anything (we never know if Thelma and Von Sternheim connect at all—the purpose established in the narrative is not resolved).

The addition of Spanky from the Our Gang series, prior to his becoming the leading player in those films, is not used to its potential. He utters a few snide remarks that are funny, but they don't contribute much and don't seem at all necessary. In fact, his part was so minimal, he had trouble recalling having done it years later. In a 1980 interview with the author, George "Spanky" McFarland stated, "I remember doing a couple of pictures set on a train. One with the gang, and one with Thelma Todd and ZaSu Pitts. I was very young and don't remember details, but do recall both women were very kind and patient with me."[24]

The fact that Spanky is referred to as ZaSu's little brother seems like a rather loose reason for him to be here. His character serves very little purpose and distracts from the main narrative, but, as stated, the film is not well-structured and gags come and go without flowing into each other. It is unfortunate that the last Pitts–Todd short was less interesting than their immediately previous efforts.

Filming on this short ended in March 1933, after which Roach closed the studio for the usual vacation, with plans to reopen on June 1. During this time, Thelma flew to England to promote *The Devil's Brother*, a Laurel and Hardy feature released just prior to *One Track Minds*. Thelma played a supporting role in this feature as the love interest for operatic singer Dennis King. She enjoyed making appearances with King and frequent Laurel and Hardy supporting comedian James Finlayson, who was also in the film. While in England, Thelma took on a movie role that she enjoyed, as she felt it extended her appeal to international cinema: She played the female lead opposite Stanley Lupino in the feature *You Made Me Love You*. While making this film, Thelma collapsed and was examined by a doctor, who indicated that she did not have a strong heart and may not live a long life. This was already known, as Thelma had been diagnosed with a heart murmur some years before and was prone to fainting spells. Some insiders felt this could have been brought on by stress due to her often difficult marriage to Pat De Cicco.

After she recovered, Thelma went to Glasgow, Scotland, by train, continuing to promote the Laurel and Hardy movie. Also on the train was Albert Einstein, who was to receive an honorary degree in Glasgow. A fan of Einstein's writings, Thelma was very pleased to meet him. However, the professor was arriving a day earlier than he had been expected, so the massive throng of greeters where the train stopped were all there for Thelma. There were so many, Thelma was concerned that someone might get hurt in the raucous crowd. Reporters were a bit chagrined that she, a mere film actress, received so much attention while the prestigious Mr. Einstein received so little. They didn't bother to consider the fact that it was because Einstein was a day early. Thelma tried to maintain some semblance of good humor, stating, "I don't know anything about relativity, but I can give people a laugh, and that's something Einstein can't do."[25] It was supposed to be funny, but the Glasgow newspapers were incensed, believing the actress was speaking condescendingly toward the prestigious professor. The Glasgow papers started predicting Thelma's current stardom would be short-lived.

While all of this was going on, ZaSu Pitts was negotiating her contract with Hal Roach. The May 19, 1933, issue of *The Hollywood Reporter* stated:

> The Hal Roach organization is planning to cut its program for the new year down to about 40 pictures. The company made 52 on its old program. The Taxi Boys comedies has been dropped and indications at this time are that there will not be another Pitts–Todd series. Thelma Todd has been signed, but the company has been unable to get together with ZaSu Pitts on another deal. Thelma Todd, however, is scheduled for eight shorts, another comedy player to be engaged to co-star with her in the event the Pitts deal fails to materialize before the studio re-opens on June 1st. New personalities will be seen in 1933–34 shorts. Already signed are Patsy Kelly, Don Barclay, Douglas Wakefield and Billy Nelson.[26]

A follow-up article in the June 3, 1933 *Hollywood Reporter* announced plans to resume production: "Henry Ginsberg, general manager, announced that negotiations with ZaSu Pitts for another group of two-reel comedies, co-starring with Thelma Todd, have been dropped. Studio declined to meet the player's demand for $8000 per picture. Patsy Kelly will replace her."[27]

While in retrospect we now realize this transition was successful, at the time it was quite a disruption. The Thelma–ZaSu comedies were pretty firmly established, and while Thelma would be continuing, Hal Roach didn't like losing someone the caliber of Pitts, who brought a further dimension to the comedies and had a name that audiences recognized. However, Roach did see the potential in Patsy Kelly and believed she would work nicely with Thelma. Roach was fully aware that Thelma was a strong and versatile performer who could work with just about anyone. He believed this teaming would work out well. And, once again, Hal Roach was correct.

4

The Films of Thelma Todd
and Patsy Kelly

Beauty and the Bus (1933)

Directed by Gus Meins; *Produced by* Hal Roach; *Cinematographer:* Hap Depew; *Editor:* William Terhune; *Cast:* Thelma Todd, Patsy Kelly, Don Barclay, Eddie Baker, Tiny Sandford, Ernie Alexander, Tommy Bond, Charlie Hall, Robert McKenzie, Jack Hill; *Released by* MGM on September 16, 1933; Two Reels

Beauty and the Bus was the first teaming of Thelma Todd and Patsy Kelly.

Patsy was born Sarah Veronica Rose Kelly on January 12, 1910, to Irish immigrants Jon and Delia Kelly. She was given the nickname Patsy by her brother. She recalled in an interview with Dena Reed, "I was in the hospital more than I was out of it as a result of street accidents, so my mother thought the best way to keep me out of mischief and use up my energy was to let me take tap-dancing lessons. I began when I was nine."[1]

Patsy started working on the vaudeville stage at age 12 and eventually joined vaudevillian Frank Fay's act, doing both music and comedy. Fay eventually developed a romantic interest in Patsy. While Patsy is noted as being among the few openly gay performers in 1930s films, she did not reveal her sexuality to Fay when she rejected his advances. This cooled their relationship, and Patsy was fired for addressing him by his first name rather than as Mr. Fay.

Patsy made her Broadway debut in 1928, and also performed in Earl Carroll's *Vanities*. She appeared in a Vitaphone short in 1931, but most of her success in the early 1930s was on Broadway. Patsy told Reed, "I used to spend my money as fast as I made it. I was always flat broke. I swore that I'd never go into pictures. Well, during one of the periods when I was 'flat,' Hal Roach and Howard Dietz talked me into signing a contract, and before I came to I was on my way to Hollywood."

Kelly was finishing work in the Broadway musical *Flying Colors* and Thelma Todd was in London, but by June 1933 the two were both at the Roach Studios ready to team up to continue Thelma's two-reel comedy series. Patsy recalled for the author in 1976, "I was hesitant because it is always hard to replace somebody that everyone loved. But Thelma was terrific, the production people welcomed me, and even ZaSu came to the studio and helped coach me. They couldn't have been nicer."[2]

Pitts was kind enough to assist in toning Patsy's theater instincts down. Theater acting is very broad, playing to an audience that reaches back many rows and up into the balcony. The movie camera is more intimate and catches the slightest nuance. And although the slapstick of the Roach comedies was very broad, Patsy still needed to temper her performance for the camera. ZaSu helped her do that.

The teaming of Todd and Kelly certainly offers the viewer something different from the Todd–Pitts comedies. While ZaSu was forlorn, Patsy was brassy. Where ZaSu was shy, Patsy was gregarious. This new dynamic was actually as funny, or arguably even funnier, and the films uniformly as good or better.

Patsy's personality and how it plays off of Todd's is immediately exhibited with the opening scene of *Beauty and the Bus*. The girls enter a theater where a car is being given away at a raffle. Patsy manages to slip on a roller skate, and catches a man's feet in the back opening of her chair as she sits down. Throughout this, she offers a running commentary of snappy wisecracks, and challenges the man behind her by demanding, "Put your foot where it belongs." He replies, "Don't tempt me!" Thelma must hold her back from commenting further.

In the earlier films, Thelma is the wiseacre and ZaSu is the meeker counterpart. Here both girls are wiseacres and Patsy is actually more aggressive than Thelma. When they win the auto and are pulled over for speeding, Thelma is the one who flirts, while Patsy's mouth almost gets them both in trouble. Each girl is grounded, secure and boisterous, but it is Patsy who refers to the cop as a "flatfoot" and a "big palooka!"

One thing Patsy does have in common with ZaSu is the ability to make impulsive mistakes. During the raffle, the theater owner calls out the number 108 as the winner. Patsy looks at her tickets and sees none match, so she tosses them away. When the theater owner realizes he is holding his paper upside down and the winner is actually 801, Thelma excitedly tells Patsy that is one of their tickets, so they must crawl about the floor and find it. Patsy and ZaSu appear to possess some of the same level of clumsiness that works well against Thelma's straight character, but Patsy is confident, even if her confidence is misplaced, whereas ZaSu was not. It makes for a different but still effective dynamic.

Patsy's aggressive behavior is further revealed when a motorist bumps them from behind. They pull over and start arguing, and Patsy starts ripping apart the man's car; the man retaliates. One is reminded of Laurel and Hardy's 1928 silent classic *Two Tars* which made an entire two-reel comedy based on this concept. Here it is not quite as artful, but utilizes the same idea. Soon a burly truck driver, with a vehicle full of furniture, gets involved in the fracas. He fights with the other motorist and proceeds to totally destroy Thelma and Patsy's car thinking it belongs to the other motorist. When Thelma finally tells him his error, he is contrite, but looks up to find Patsy atop his truck,

Left to right: Don Barclay with Thelma Todd and, making her debut, Patsy Kelly in *Beauty and the Bus* (1933).

76

throwing the furniture onto the street. The truck driver begs her to stop. As with the Laurel and Hardy film, several cars end up creating a massive traffic jam.

The scene switches to Thelma and Patsy pushing their car along a path, being again confronted by the previous motorist, resulting in their new car flying into the ocean. They throw the other motorist in the water and take over his car. However, Thelma drives and makes Patsy run alongside. Patsy pleads, "Come on, palsie-walsie! Have I ever caused you any trouble?"

Despite this being their first film together, Thelma and Patsy already have on-screen chemistry and, despite Patsy getting Thelma into trouble, there is a warmth between them that makes it appear that they have been longtime friends. The car going into the water initially seems a rather clichéd ending to an otherwise quite funny comedy, but the girls reacting by throwing the other driver into the water and then stealing *his* car is a neat twist. Their team dynamic is presented when they gang up to toss him in the water, and is challenged with Thelma kicking Patsy out of the car and making her walk.

Variety announced in its August 8, 1933, issue that Billy Gilbert would direct the film, which is puzzling in that by August this film would have been completed filming and in post-production. All signs point to Gus Meins helming this short, having often directed the Todd and Pitts films. He responds to the new team dynamic successfully. Meins had a good eye for visual humor and is able to shoot the traffic jam creatively, showing it via close-ups of the wheels from several cars slamming into one another.

Roach was pleased with the final product and Patsy was offered a contract. But she was overwhelmed by the physical demands of the comedy and decided not to continue with the series. She told the author in 1976:

> I was a nervous wreck. The very first day I told the director that he should maybe get a stunt double for some of my scenes and he laughed his head off. He thought I must be joking. We finished the picture and I had it. It was back to the theater for me. Thelma talked me out of it and eventually I got the hang of it. Everybody was so supportive. The Hal Roach studio was the greatest place I ever worked.

Although Patsy agreed to continue working with Thelma in the Roach comedies and signed a contract, filming had to be postponed before her next movie. Two weeks after wrapping production on *Beauty and the Bus*, Patsy was involved in an automobile accident in which she was injured and her friend, entertainer Jean Malin, was killed. Malin is noted as being among the first openly gay performers; his specialty was female impersonation. He was quite popular in nightclubs and stage revues, and well liked by fellow performers. Malin was driving the car in which his partner, Jimmy Forlenza, and friend Patsy were passengers. The car was parked outside of a club against a safety block on a pier. Weary from having just performed, Malin confused the gears and threw the car into reverse instead of first. It went off the pier, hurdling the safety block and plunging into the water. Malin, 25, was killed, Patsy and Forlenza injured.

Patsy was submerged in the water long enough to suffer both shock and other critical injuries. A citizen heard her cries for help, dove into the water and rescued her in time. Forlenza had been thrown from the car before it went into the water and suffered a broken collarbone. It was determined that Malin did not drown, but had been killed by the impact itself. His body was pinned beneath the steering wheel.

Patsy was ready to return to the film series after two weeks of recovery. Although she survived, doctors told Patsy that she would only live another ten years due to sand that had seeped into her lungs. Patsy vowed to make the most of the little time she had left. She did not know that she would actually live another 48 years.

Backs to Nature (1933)

Directed by Gus Meins; *Produced by* Hal Roach; *Cinematographer:* Francis Corby; *Editor:* Louis McManus; *Cast:* Thelma Todd, Patsy Kelly, Don Barclay, Alice Belcher, Charlie Hall, Baldwin Cooke; *Released by* MGM on November 14, 1933; Two Reels

Once Patsy Kelly had healed up from injuries sustained in the car crash and was able to go back to work in the comedies, preparations were quickly made. In the October 6, 1933, *Film Daily*, this blurb appeared: "Gus Meins, Hal Roach director, is a great lover of the outdoors. For *Backs to Nature* featuring Thelma Todd and Patsy Kelly, he desired an ideal camp site. He made an extensive search and ended up having the "camp" built in the studio."[3]

Meins, with his noted visual sense, made it appear that the camping scenes were authentic despite sets that often made it obvious that shooting was indoors on a soundstage.

In this one, Thelma and Patsy are working at a baggage claim, dealing with all manner of customers, from a bootlegger whose heavy bag is dropped by Patsy and causes the bottles therein to shatter, to the organ grinder wanting to check a bag containing his live monkey (who naturally escapes, causing the scene to end in tumult). Patsy and Thelma want to truly get away during their much-needed vacation, and while Thelma would like to relax in a four-star hotel room and get served meals in bed, Patsy believes they should escape to "God's country." An entire short could likely have been made from the premise as presented in the opening sequence with the girls working in the baggage claim. But it is left behind for a comedy about roughing it in the wilderness.

What results is mostly tried-and-true stuff, with the girls becoming entangled in the ropes and canvas as they attempt to pitch a tent, Patsy chopping down a tree that naturally crashes onto the tent with Thelma in it, and a scary visit from a wandering bear.

All of the gags, however amusing they may be, are very predictable.

There are, however, some exceptionally funny moments and a few rather creative ideas. When Patsy swings an axe in an attempt to chop down a large tree, a cascade of large pinecones comes crashing on top of her. When she shuts her eyes and tries to shoot a rabbit, the buckshot makes several holes in the coffee pot Thelma is using. When they hold ears of corn over a campfire, the corn starts popping like popcorn.

Patsy is presented as the klutzy one whose enthusiastic attempts to take care of everything always end up backfiring with Thelma taking the fall. At one point, Thelma asks Patsy, "Is there any place I can go and be safe from you?" Along with her klutziness, Patsy also has a certain pride, the opposite of the forlorn ZaSu Pitts character. When Thelma has Patsy get out of the way so she can do a job correctly, Patsy responds with "That's the thanks I get for trying to be helpful." Patsy seems to have a few phrases that are repeated for comic effect, such as "Just leave everything to me" and "That could have happened to anybody."

While the chemistry is there, it appears that some growth would be necessary for the Todd–Kelly teaming to finds its way to the level that the Todd–Pitts films eventually reached. Of course it took a few films for that teaming to establish itself as well as it eventually did. Patsy, although apprehensive after the first film, was more confident with this next one. Patsy recalled for the author: "I had experience as an actress. I had a character that I usually played. I was no beginner. But I was learning how to work in pictures and how to respond to Thelma as well as the situations. It was on the job learning, so to speak." Patsy's work in these shorts would continue to be honed, while Thelma continued to anchor each scene.

As the films were being produced during the pre–Code era, there continued to be some risqué moments. *Backs to Nature's* title is based on the one

Left to right: Thelma Todd, Gus Meins and Patsy Kelly—looks like they are scouting locations on the Roach lot for *Backs to Nature* (1933).

truly edgy scene in the film, which comes at the very end. The girls climb a tree to get away from the bear, just as some foreign rangers show up and start shooting at the animal. One of the shots grazes the girls just enough to knock off their clothes. They are shown in a close-up with their bare backs to the screen as the movie ends. It's a pretty weird way to end the film, and can be perceived as more shocking than funny, even for the pre–Code era.

Backs to Nature was very well received by moviegoers, with theater owners stating that the film got plenty of laughs and went over great. None seemed to opine that ZaSu Pitts was necessary for the comedy team to continue with success. Patsy Kelly was happily accepted..

As she continued to work in these comedies, Patsy became closer friends with Thelma and more fascinated by her as an actress and a performer. They used to watch the footage they shot and laugh at each other's work, each declaring the other to be the funniest. It became a running gag between them. Patsy also was amused by Thelma's carefree attitude. Still a newcomer to film, Patsy was careful to adapt from her theater experience, especially doing comedy to no audience reaction. Thelma never took things too seriously, and would make faces at the cameraman and pull practical jokes on the set. But what really endured Thelma to Patsy, and others, was her compassion. Whenever she would work with a crew member she had spoken to a few films earlier, she always seemed to remember their children's names, etc., and ask about their well being.

Shortly after filming *Backs to Nature*, Kelly was borrowed from Roach by MGM, the studio that distributed his product, for an appearance in her first feature length movie. *Going Hollywood* was a William Randolph Hearst production featuring his mistress Marion Davies and current singing sensation Bing Crosby. Patsy shines in a supporting role, giving her even greater confidence regarding her success in movies. Still a newcomer, Kelly would very quickly establish herself as a welcome comic presence in some major feature films, and her services as an actress would be sought more and more frequently from other studios.

Thelma appeared in two features during this time, the Paramount musical *Sitting Pretty* featuring Jack Haley, Jack Oakie and Ginger Rogers, and the Warner Brothers comedy *Son of a Sailor* starring Joe E. Brown, who was at that time among the top stars in movies. When working in feature films, including the wholesome brand of cornball comedy that Brown excelled in, Thelma expanded upon her cinematic notoriety beyond the two-reelers.

Air Fright (1933)

Directed by Gus Meins; *Produced by* Hal Roach; *Cinematographer:* Kenneth Peach; *Editor:* Bert Jordan; *Cast:* Thelma Todd, Patsy Kelly, Don Barclay, Billy Bletcher, Wilfred Lucas, Gladys Blake, Sydney Jarvis, Robert McKenzie, Isabelle Keith; *Released by* MGM on November 14, 1933; Two Reels

According to reports from theater owners, audiences were pleased with the initial comedies featuring Thelma Todd with Patsy Kelly, the transition from ZaSu Pitts being a seamless one. *Air Fright*, one of the duo's funnier shorts, offers each at her best.

Thelma is an airline hostess who gets her friend Patsy a job. The boss trusts Thelma, but Patsy is someone whose impulsive behavior has to be contained. Naturally this is up to Thelma. The girls are assigned to ride in a plane that has a new device: an ejector seat where a person can drop down out of the bottom of the plane and parachute to safety. A stunt pilot is hired to do the demonstration for several potential investors who are along for the flight. Thelma carefully goes over the rules with Patsy ("The customer is always right," "Service with a smile"). Patsy's naturally aggressive demeanor conflicts with these rules, but she does her best as Thelma sneers and glares, trying to keep her in line.

Slapstick abounds. First, when the inventor of the ejector seat attempts to give an example from the ground, Patsy is standing in just the right spot to come plummeting through the bottom of the plane. When the aircraft takes off, Patsy slips out the door and has to be pulled back in. She also becomes airsick at the outset of the flight, and struggles to hand out trays. She bumps into the stunt man, causing his lit cigar to pop out of his mouth and fall into his flight suit. He hurriedly jumps out of the plane, parachutes to the ground and extricates the cigar from his suit, standing angrily in his underwear. This ruins the demonstration, so the boss tells the girls to see him in his office when the plane lands.

The comedies produced by Hal Roach always had a great counterbalance between slapstick and situational comedy, with the Charley Chase series offering more situational humor, while Laurel and Hardy would often provide two reels of slapstick gags. *Air Fright* provides some wildly funny slapstick gags that are both clever and nicely played. There is something a bit more artful in the execution of slapstick here. Perhaps it is Patsy Kelly's strong presence (compared to ZaSu Pitts' frail character) that allows for the knockabout comedy to be more effective.

The film continues as the boss makes sure the ejector seat is safe, and decides to trick Patsy into taking the stunt man's place to demonstrate the device. Patsy is assigned a seat, but she keeps excitedly getting up to look out the window, to joke with another passenger, etc., every time the ejection lever is about to be pulled. Once she finally sits, the inventor pulls the incorrect lever, causing one of the investors to plummet from the plane. Then Patsy curiously works the levers, causing each of the other investors to parachute down in their seats. All of the male investors in this scene behave in a very condescending manner toward Patsy; she plays along without really picking up on it, but it makes the part where she ejects them each, one by one, all the more satisfying.

Director Gus Meins makes each of these situations separate slapstick events. One passenger falls into a hornets' nest. Another lands on a smoky

Left to right: Patsy Kelly, Wilfred Lucas and Thelma Todd in *Air Fright* (1933).

chimney. Yet another splashes into a body of water. Then Patsy and Thelma become entangled in a parachute that is dangling from the moving plane while wrapped around the inventor's neck. When the girls finally fall, they land on railroad tracks and just miss being hit by a passing train as the film concludes.

As with many of Thelma and Patsy's two-reelers, there is no real conclusion to *Air Fright*, just a series of gags that concludes with the ejection of all of the passengers. We are not offered any subsequent conflict the girls may have with their boss. What we do get is a continued presentation of the chemistry between Thelma and Patsy.

Comedies with an aviation background date back as far as the Keystone short *A Dash Through the Clouds*. In *Air Fright*, Thelma and Patsy are not interested in becoming pilots or flying the plane, but there are ideas within the framework of their being stewardesses that offer fertile ground for slapstick ideas. Thelma is attractive, competent and ultimately frustrated as her altruism is challenged by Patsy's rough edges. The idea that the boorish, tomboyish Patsy, who has to be carefully coached to be pleasant and helpful, is going to succeed as a flight attendant is an outrageous concept. Thelma tries to keep Patsy in line, but she has her own responsibilities, and some of the sudden actions can't be caught in time to prevent. Thelma's reactions, her bulging eyes and slow burns, are not dissimilar to those exhibited by Oliver Hardy, of Roach's popular team of Laurel and Hardy, when he is comically frustrated. Just as it is often Stan Laurel who creates the chaos in one of their films, Patsy is the culprit here. The comic reactions from their respective partners have similarities. While Patsy's character is noisier and more central, Thelma's quieter presence never seems to be overshadowed by her more boisterous partner.

The continued favorable response to the shorts gave Patsy more confidence and she continued to feel more and more comfortable working in the comedies. "It was pretty rough most of the time," she recalled in a 1976 interview with the author, "slapstick comedy hurts! But I was surrounded by such great people who were always ready to be supportive, that I guess I just got used to it."

Kelly made no films away from the Roach studios after completing *Air Fright*, but Todd was characteristically busy. At Universal she had a supporting role in the John Barrymore feature *Counsellor-at-Law*, then another supporting role in the indie feature *Palooka* featuring Jimmy Durante, Lupe Velez and Stuart Erwin, and then headed to RKO for a larger role with Bert Wheeler and Robert Woolsey in *Hips Hips Hooray*. In the latter film, Thelma tapped into other areas of her comic skills: The female lead in the movie, she is billed above Wheeler and Woolsey's usual female player Dorothy Lee. (But Ruth Etting is billed above Thelma, and just after the starring comic duo, despite only singing one song for roughly three minutes of screen time.)

There was talk of doing a live touring show called *Dumb Bells*, written by Tim Whelan. It would feature Wheeler and Woolsey, along with Thelma Todd and Dorothy Lee. Unfortunately, it never materialized.

The day before this film was released, November 13, 1933, *Film Daily* announced in its "News of the Day" column that Hal Roach renewed Kelly's contract through the Ralph G. Farnum Office.

Babes in the Goods (1934)

Directed by Gus Meins; *Produced by* Hal Roach; *Cinematographer:* Kenneth Peach; *Editor:* Louis McManus; *Cast:* Thelma Todd, Patsy Kelly, Jack

Barty, Arthur Housman, Fay Holderness, Carl M. Leviness, Charlie Hall, Charley Rogers, Charlton Griffin, Baldwin Cooke, Jack Hill; *Released by* MGM on February 10, 1934; Two Reels

The dynamic that had shifted since ZaSu Pitts left the act continues to flourish with *Babes in the Goods*, another Todd–Kelly comedy that seeks to further refine their relationship.

This time the girls are department store workers who can't manage to make a sale. Weary, they are asked to replace the two women displaying a washing machine in the store's window. They are told that they must continue the display while there is anyone watching. They end up getting locked in the store overnight, with an interested party watching their every move.

There are many aspects to *Babes in the Goods* that make it a particularly good comedy. First, Thelma and Patsy are selling nightgowns to a very demanding woman with a baby. There are some nice bits of humor with Thelma taking the potential sale a bit more seriously, while Patsy has a hard time modeling the nightgowns and then is asked to hold the woman's baby while she shops

When the two girls demonstrate in the storefront window, they are ogled by the males on the street, especially when one of the ladies bends to pick something up. There is a neat shot from behind where the crowd moves along with the woman as she bends, director Gus Meins framing the action with his usual aplomb.

Once Thelma and Patsy are on duty in the storefront window, they pretty much make a shambles of the entire display, with water spraying toward the window and everyone on the street ducking even though the window keeps them from getting wet. It is all about voyeurism from this point on. The shot of the crowd watching and laughing mirrors ourselves viewing the comedy, allowing us to share in their reaction. Once the crowd disperses, just one man remains, a drunk fascinated by the presentation. Having to keep active while he watches, the very tired girls finally put up the store curtains hoping he will go away. He does not, and watches their shadows against the shade. He sees Thelma strip to her negligee, causing him to back up into a trash can!

Much of the comedy is pretty standard, involving Thelma and Patsy trying to settle for the night in the bed display after having been locked in. It is at this point that the film starts to plod along and offer little. Things pick up when the sun rises and a crowd again gathers. Thelma is seen in her underwear, and a door slams on Patsy's dress, putting her on the same level of undress. They wrap themselves in blankets to cover up, but when the boss arrives and fires them, they must leave the covers behind and again reveal their state of undress.

Significantly, the girls don't leave ashamed: They walk out proudly and on their own terms. When they throw down the blankets and walk off, the boss, who didn't know that they weren't wearing any clothes underneath, is shocked and put in an awkward position having that sort of risqué display in his store window.

It is interesting to see the progression of Thelma and Patsy's on-screen relationship. The earlier films had Patsy holding her own within the parameters of a comedy team; as the comedies continued, she began to hone her character. While she was immediately more aggressive than the forlorn ZaSu Pitts, there are layers of Kelly's character development that appear in each successive film. In these same situations, ZaSu would be embarrassed and appalled, whereas Patsy is more confrontational, frequently asking, "Wanna make somethin' out of it?" as part of her basic character.

While it is not terribly likely that Alfred Hitchcock's voyeuristic classic *Rear Window* (1954) was at all influenced by this comedy short, *Babes in the*

Patsy Kelly and Thelma Todd in *Babes in the Goods* (1934).

86

Goods does approach the concept in its own way. A crowd is watching Thelma and Patsy's mishaps the same as we, the viewers, are. It soon settles down to only one man, fascinated by the idea of a living display, despite his inebriation (which is part of actor Arthur Housman's comic persona in most of his film appearances). Initially the girls have an assignment, but they mess that up in comic fashion, much to the delight of the onlookers. They then are allowed some respite when they must sleep in the window, after being locked in. The curtains that hide the merchandise overnight are open as they awaken. The drunk is back, the crowd returns as well, and the scantily clad girls are fired before all of them.

Film Daily called *Babes in the Goods* "hilarious ... packed with laughs."[4] *Motion Picture Daily* considered the film "plenty of fun" and pointed out that there was "quite some lingerie displayed."[5] Audiences delighted in the films, and Hal Roach was pleased with the effectiveness of this new team dynamic.

Gus Meins continued to spotlight each actress, and their cohesion as a team, gradually honing a formula. The transition from ZaSu Pitts to Patsy Kelly was now complete. It almost appeared as if the right shots, the best edits and the most effective angles was second nature to Meins, as he continued to explore the possibilities of each film.

Shortly after completing *Babes in the Goods*, Todd went to Universal for a supporting role in the feature film *The Poor Rich*. Kelly got the second female lead in the Universal feature *The Countess of Monte Cristo*, a film with Fay Wray in the title role (a small-time actress trying to convince others that she is, in fact, royalty). Critics stated that Patsy stole the film from Wray and a formidable cast that also included Paul Lukas and Reginald Owen.

Noticing her success, Roach wondered if, in fact, both Patsy and Thelma would do better as solo performers. Thelma had already proven herself many times as an actress at the studio, but now Patsy seemed to have quite formidable skills as well. It was something the producer felt was worth pondering.

Soup and Fish (1934)

Directed by Gus Meins; *Produced by* Hal Roach; *Cinematographer:* Francis Corby; *Editor:* Louis McManus; *Cast:* Thelma Todd, Patsy Kelly, Gladys Gale, Billy Gilbert, Don Barclay, Ernie Alexander, Baldwin Cooke, Charlie Hall, Virginia Karns, Alphonse Martell, Eric Manye, Elinor Vanderveer; *Released by* MGM on March 31, 1934; Two Reels

The films of Thelma Todd and Patsy Kelly settled into a consistent formula. While the chemistry between them was always discernible, even in their first short, the rough edges of their relationship, differing significantly from the one Todd had with ZaSu Pitts, needed to be sharpened. The duo benefiting from having the same director, Gus Meins, over several productions.

Soup and Fish draws from their characters, and their on-screen relationship, more effectively than their previous comedies. Thelma and Patsy work at a ritzy salon. Mrs. Dukesbery, a haughty woman with a doting chauffeur who stands by and holds her pampered dog, is having a mudpack treatment. Unable to see clearly, she believes she is inviting two fellow society women to a gathering at her home, when she is in fact asking Thelma and Patsy to attend. The reason for the gathering is to introduce a visiting count to American society.

Within this framework, we have Thelma, excited about the prospect of bettering her station with more entitled acquaintances who operate at a societal level far above her own, and down-to-earth Patsy, who has no interest in putting on airs, and merely wants to have fun with a few practical joke novelties. As they approach the mansion in rented gowns, Patsy shakes Thelma's hand with a joy buzzer. Thelma tells her to be on her best behavior. Mrs. Dukesbery has been called away to the animal hospital where her dog is staying, so the girls are welcomed as invited guests.

This set-up offers a great canvas on which Todd and Kelly can create a lot of good comic situations. Patsy walks in with confidence, making cracks about a butler's short pants, snarkily commenting on others at the party, even responding incorrectly to Dukesbery's daughter who indicates that the woman of the house is at the animal hospital. When Patsy is told she is looking after her dogs, Patsy (referring to her feet) says, "Mine are killing me too!" Patsy exhibits boorish table etiquette while sitting next to the visiting count. While Thelma fumes, the count actually is amused by Patsy's demeanor and laughs at her jokes. As Thelma becomes more and more frustrated by her friend's behavior, the count finds Patsy more and more endearing.

This idea was used in other comedies before and after *Soup and Fish*. An invited guest whose behavior is comparatively atrocious is perceived by some members of the upper crust as down-to-earth and more attractive than the severe limitations of the good manners that come from proper breeding. The Three Stooges, for instance, explored this idea in *Hoi Polloi* (1935) and *Half-Wits Holiday* (1946) in which they are part of an experiment to see if proper etiquette instruction can refine people from the lowest strata in life. In *Hoi Polloi*, party guests suddenly begin slapping and eye-poking each other in Stooges fashion. *Half-Wits Holiday* concludes with a massive pie fight.

The approach in this earlier Roach production is different. Patsy's practical jokes cause all manner of disruption, culminating when she puts a toy mechanical mouse on the table, wreaking havoc as it motors past the guests. This prompts the butler to call Dukesbery, who rushes home. When she arrives, the count and another partygoer are crawling along the floor pushing a peanut with their noses in a race. Appalled, Dukesbery orders Thelma and Patsy to leave. The count stops her, insisting that he's having the most fun he's had in years.

Poster for *Soup and Fish* (1934).

In her earlier films with ZaSu Pitts, Thelma Todd would usually lead the proceedings with ZaSu the hapless follower. Here Patsy holds her own, her boisterous manner breaking away from Thelma's influence. The dynamic features the aggressive personality of Patsy being central to the narrative and Thelma as the more grounded personality who tries to temper her friend's behavior. This works nicely. While the duo had made funny films all along, *Soup to Fish* is probably the best checkpoint as to where their characters really seemed to be fully established as a working comedy unit.

Billy Gilbert's versatility at Roach is once again evident in his role as the count. Gilbert could play everything from lower-class louts to pretentious upper-class society figures, and everything in between. He could be gruff, ingratiating, forceful or prissy. In *Soup and Nuts* he is placed within the pretentious world of society types, but his attraction is to the one ordinary working class type (Patsy Kelly's character). It is really quite delightful.

Gilbert is the only supporting actor to offer a lot to this film. The others are amusing, but in smaller spurts, almost decorative in their comic approach. Don Barclay worked often with Todd and Kelly, and registers amusingly as one of the servants. But the others are fleeting, bolstering the scenes as guests, or beauty parlor customers, but given little to do.

Gus Meins once again goes beyond the usual directorial style for two-reel comedies by using some good visuals to enhance the various scenes. For instance, as Patsy is cavorting boorishly at the head of the table during dinner, Meins cuts away to a deep focus shot of the long table of society types, all looking incredulously toward the camera (at Patsy). It is a nice touch that makes the proceedings that much more amusing.

By 1934, the notorious Production Code started to be enforced more rigorously, so the more risqué elements of the comedies during the pre–Code period were no longer utilized. The comedy came from character, situations and gags. Slapstick continued to be central, and the characters of the two women, and their relationship, had been honed to perfection.

However, Hal Roach continued to ponder the possibility of using Thelma and Patsy as separate solo performers. So while Thelma was away from the studio filming the Spencer Tracy starrer *Bottoms Up* at Fox, Roach experimented with Patsy in her own solo film: *Roamin' Vandals* has Patsy in the lead, with support from actress Lillian Miles. They are traveling with a medicine show headed by Billy Gilbert. As usual, Patsy's boisterous manner and bad temper keep getting her into trouble. In every town, she seems to get into fights, alerting the sheriff and forcing the show to hastily leave town. A tangent is introduced where a stereotypical Indian character wants to make Patsy his squaw. The film ends with a comic chase scene. While *Roamin' Vandals* was very well received by moviegoers, Roach apparently thought better of breaking up the team, and hereafter the two women remained a duo.

Maid in Hollywood (1934)

Directed by Gus Meins; *Produced by* Hal Roach; *Cinematographer:* Francis Corby; *Editor:* Louis McManus; *Stunt Double for Don Barclay:* Ed Brandenburg; *Cast:* Thelma Todd, Patsy Kelly, Constance Bergen, Don Barclay,

Eddie Foy, Jr., Billy Gilbert, Jack Barty, Alphonse Martell, Dick Gilbert, Harry Bernard, Billy Bletcher, Carlton Griffin, Charlie Hall, James C. Morton, Billy Nelson, Charley Rogers, Ted Storback, Betty Danko, Pat West; *Released by* MGM on May 19, 1934; Two Reels

Screen comedy often parodied itself, and *Maid in Hollywood* is a good satire on the motion picture industry.

Thelma and Patsy are living in a Hollywood rooming house. Thelma is distraught that they have been there for some time and she has not broken into movies as she'd planned. The girls decide to return to their home town, when a neighbor stops by to proudly assert that she has a screen test scheduled. Without Thelma's knowledge, Patsy locks this woman in a closet; she then calls the studio and says that this woman cannot make it to the screen test and suggests they instead try Thelma. Desperate, the studio agrees. When Thelma gets a call from the studio to report, she is ecstatic.

Thelma excitedly leaves for the studio, and insists Patsy remain home. However, when Patsy sees that Thelma has forgotten her makeup kit, she brings it to the studio. She stays and causes a series of problems during Thelma's screen test. Despite all of this, Thelma ends up getting the part.

A consistent series of mishaps, *Maid in Hollywood* draws equally from slapstick gags, situational humor, the charm of the central characters, and support of the cast. It is one of the strongest Todd–Kelly comedies.

At the outset, the film examines the relationship between the characters a bit more deeply. Thelma is despondent and Patsy is appropriately wise-cracking until she realizes how truly depressed her friend is. Patsy then is uncharacteristically warm and understanding. This very serious look at the girls' predicament and their relationship is uncharacteristic, but very effective. For once, Thelma appears to need Patsy, rather than the other way around. Meanwhile, the girl who boasts of her screen test is so haughty and pretentious, that Patsy's locking her in the closet comes off as triumphantly amusing rather than like bullying.

On the set, Thelma emerges in a beautiful gown like the one she wore in the Laurel and Hardy costume feature *The Devil's Brother*. The film then wavers between Thelma valiantly trying to do her lines and secure the part, and Patsy's noisy attempts to be helpful. There is a running gag where Patsy continually snags her foot on the cord connected to the sound equipment, causing it to all come crashing to the floor. Patsy also walks directly into a scene as it is being filmed, and starts telling Thelma how great she looks. When Thelma has trouble sneezing during another sequence, Patsy recalls how a breeze from an open window caused her to do so in the apartment earlier. So Patsy turns on a fan to create such a breeze, not realizing it is placed right next to where some open pepper is placed. The seasoning flies about the set, causing *everyone* to start sneezing.

During this outrageously funny sneezing sequence, director Gus Meins cuts to a few specific incidents as punctuating gags. For instance, there is one shot of a man sneezing his dentures out. There is a big sneeze, followed by a shot of a set of teeth still clenching a cigar. Meins presents it so that the gag enhances the scene but does not distract from the film's stars.

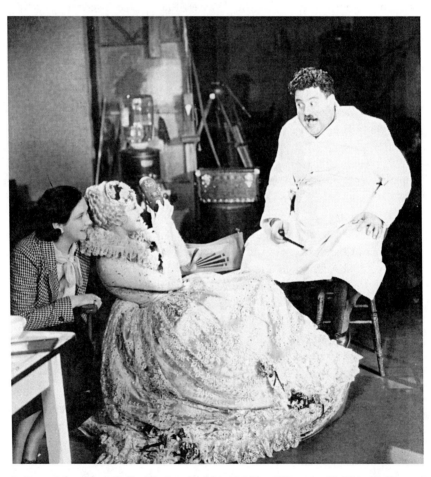

Left to right: Patsy Kelly, Thelma Todd and Billy Gilbert in *Maid in Hollywood* (1934).

With all of the physical comedy in *Maid in Hollywood*, there is also a great deal of character nuance. For instance, during Thelma's attempt to sneeze, Billy Gilbert, playing a deli man making a delivery, is summoned. Gilbert, a comedian who specialized in comic sneezes (he would later voice the character of Sneezy in Walt Disney's *Snow White and the Seven Dwarfs* [1936]), helps bolster the scene with a German accent and his sneezing tutorial. As we've noted throughout this text, Gilbert appeared often in the Todd–Pitts and Todd–Kelly comedies, and frequently bolstered the humor any time he was on camera.

Another highlight occurs when the screen test calls for a prop gun. The prop man searches frantically for it as Patsy stands nearby holding it. Moving quickly, checking each item among the props, the property manager looks at Patsy, who holds out the gun and asks, "Is this it?" The prop man quickly answers, "No!" then does a double-take and snatches it from her hand. Of course something so quick and nuanced is far better seen than described, but it is one of many such moments that makes *Maid in Hollywood* especially amusing. The property man is played by English-born Charley Rogers, a friend of Stan Laurel's who appeared in many Roach comedies. Rogers had another amusing role in the next Todd–Kelly film, *I'll Be Suing You*. The cast is rounded out by familiar Roach character actors Eddie Foy, Jr., Charlie Hall and Don Barclay.

One interesting bit of casting is Alphonse Martell as the director. Although he appeared in nearly 300 roles in movies and on television (often in small, uncredited parts), this is his only appearance in a Hal Roach production. As the director, Martell exhibits a more serious control over the proceedings. Surrounded by funny people doing funny things, Martell is the anchor of each scene, commanding attention by exhibiting patience and support, as he appears to genuinely want Thelma to do well enough to secure the role in his movie.

The two-reeler ends on a gag. As a triumphant Thelma is returning home with Patsy, she wonders why the actress originally set for the screen test backed out. As Patsy walks by the janitor's hall closet, she casually unlocks the door and out pops the angry actress. As Thelma acknowledges it was Patsy who locked the woman up, a mop comes flying from off screen, hitting Patsy in the head and knocking her out of the frame.

Maid in Hollywood was one of the most popular Todd–Kelly comedies, and Roach was pleased with the number of bookings it secured. In the trades, theater managers commented on how their audiences laughed through it, and indicated that the Todd–Kelly series had a good number of fans. Thelma and Patsy had two more comedies to finish on their current contract, and Roach had already decided to re-sign them to eight more.

I'll Be Suing You (1934)

Directed by Gus Meins; *Produced by* Hal Roach; *Cinematographer:* Kenneth Peach; *Editor:* Louis McManus; *Cast:* Thelma Todd, Patsy Kelly, Benny Baker, Eddie Foy, Jr., Fred Kelsey, Sam Lufkin, Charles McAvoy, Billy Nelson, Charley Rogers, William Wagner, Douglas Wakefield; *Released by* MGM on June 23, 1934; Two Reels

After turning out one of their best subjects, *Maid in Hollywood*, Todd and Kelly next did the rather unremarkable *I'll Be Suing You*. The set-up seems promising: Patsy and Thelma are talked into faking an injury to collect insurance money. But the resulting film features only a few rather minor amusing moments.

Eddie Foy, Jr., who worked with the duo on several other occasions, appears as a fast-talking lawyer who comes up with the scheme for Patsy to fake a broken leg and fool a couple of insurance adjusters. Thelma goes along with the idea. But Patsy rebels, as usual, constantly saying things like "Nothin' doin'" as Thelma and Eddie work hard to set up the scene that might convince the adjusters. Of course the scheme backfires as the two-reeler concludes.

The film opens with the girls getting in a car accident. Eddie arrives at the scene and quickly tells the girls he can get them a $50,000 settlement if one of them pretends to be injured. Patsy protests, insisting she is okay, but Eddie and Thelma claim that she has been hurt. Once they are in the girls' apartment, their bed is rigged so that Patsy can stick her leg through a hole, so that it is only showing up to the knee. A mannequin leg is then placed from the knee down to give the impression of an injury.

There is a funny sequence when Charley Rogers arrives to fix the telephone. The women mistake him for an insurance adjuster, so Thelma goes into her rehearsed spiel while Charley listens quietly and starts pulling out the various tools he will need to work on the phone. The tools include saws and other rather dangerous-looking items, and the girls react as if they were implements to work on Patsy's leg. But this is really the film's only highlight. Other gags, such as a dog pulling the sock off Patsy's foot under the bed, and then licking her toes to cause a ticklish reaction in front of the insurance adjusters, are only mildly amusing.

This same gag was re-used by Our Gang in their comedy *Fishy Tales* (1937). In that film, Alfalfa pretends to have a busted-up leg to get out of a scheduled fight with bully Butch Bond. They do the same bit with Alfalfa sticking his leg through a hole in the bed, but they replace the missing portion with a large fish in a knee sock that matches the stocking on his other foot. Alfalfa's dangling foot is tickled under the bed by Junior Jasquar with a feather, and then a crab latches onto his toe, making his giggling turn to yelling in pain. The results are somewhat more amusing in the kids' comedy.

One problem with *I'll Be Suing You* is that Thelma and Patsy do not really work as a cohesive team, but seem to be two actors co-starring in a comedy short. Thelma is really given little to do. Patsy is showcased, and while she is usually funny, her noisy boisterousness needs to be tempered with Thelma's more grounded approach. Here it is not. For instance, as Thelma is describing what happened to them in the accident, Patsy punctu-

Left to right: Director Gus Meins, Patsy Kelly, Thelma Todd and Eddie Foy, Jr., on the set of *I'll Be Suing You* (1934).

95

ates the narrative with loud moans and groans. They aren't funny. They come off as annoying.

Fred Kelsey and William Wagner appear as the no-nonsense insurance adjusters. A delightfully gruff presence in several comedies, Kelsey had been appearing sporadically in Roach productions since the silent era. Working with Charley Chase most frequently, he was especially good in *The Laurel and Hardy Murder Case* (1930). When that short was remade at Columbia by the Three Stooges as *If a Body Meets a Body* 16 years later, Kelsey repeated his role.

I'll Be Suing You was disappointing, especially since Thelma and Patsy had generated screen chemistry almost from the outset of their teaming, and had honed their formula to the point where they were starting to make some of their best comedies. *Variety* was spot-on with their November 20, 1934, review:

> If Hal Roach wants Thelma Todd and Patsy Kelly to click as a team, he'd better revamp his story department and see to it that these gals get material they can sink their teeth into. They deserve a better break than they got in this one. They're a pair of good troupers, but the stuff handed them is old and devoid of laughs. If a bit more originality had been put into it, it would have been a wow. As it is, it just about rates "fair."[6]

Exhibitors were split between indicating that their audiences laughed all the way through *I'll Be Suing You*, and being disappointed. One theater owner called it their worst so far. Another called it their best.

About a month before *I'll Be Suing You* was released, Gus Meins was offered a new contract to keep directing films at Roach, securing a bigger payday for his fine work. Meins had not only been effective with the Todd–Kelly comedies, he also directed successfully for Charley Chase, the Taxi Boys and Our Gang since joining Roach a year earlier. While his end with Hal Roach would be unhappy (as would the end of his life), at this time his career was quite successful.

In June 1934, Patsy Kelly's option was renewed (along with actor Benny Baker, who also appears in *I'll Be Suing You*). Patsy had more than proven herself as a formidable replacement for ZaSu and had made her own niche in the comedies with Thelma Todd.

After completing *I'll Be Suing You*, Thelma went to RKO to once again appear with Bert Wheeler and Robert Woolsey in another one of their feature comedies. Like her previous movie with that duo, *Hips Hips Hooray*, *Cockeyed Cavaliers* was one of Wheeler and Woolsey's best films. It was a costume picture, just as Laurel and Hardy's *The Devil's Brother* had been, so Thelma looked especially beautiful while turning in a typically great performance.

Three Chumps Ahead (1934)

Directed by Gus Meins; *Produced by* Hal Roach; *Cinematographer:* Kenneth Peach; *Editor:* Louis McManus; *Cast:* Thelma Todd, Patsy Kelly Eddie Phillips, Benny Baker, Frank Moran, Ernie Adams, Ernie Alexander, Baldwin Cooke, Billy Bletcher, Harry Bernard; *Released by* MGM on July 14, 1934; Two Reels

Rebounding from the lackluster *I'll Be Suing You*, Todd and Kelly once again explore their relationship for effective comedy in *Three Chumps Ahead*. Thelma allows a rather obvious phony suitor to distract her, while Patsy sees him for the charlatan he truly is.

Now that the Todd–Kelly on-screen relationship has been established, the women can explore it with more depth. The premise of this two-reeler shows how much Thelma desires a life at a higher level, but the more realistic Patsy is grounded and suspicious. The comedy is largely situational while also being character-driven, and punctuated by slapstick gags.

The film opens with a gag: Patsy is on a ladder in front of the apartment door when Thelma bursts in, knocking her down. Thelma excitedly tells Patsy that she has met a real gentleman, Archie, and has asked him to come over. Patsy is skeptical, but the romantic Thelma is ready to believe anything.

There is an amusing scene where Thelma, with Archie's impending visit in mind, insists that Patsy remove her comfortable house slippers and squeeze into Thelma's too-small dress shoes. Then Thelma tries to coach Patsy's down-to-earth exuberance by having her rehearse how she will greet him. Thelma goes into the closet, playing the part of Archie, and comes out to see how Patsy reacts. She is too boisterous so they prepare to do it again. Archie comes to the door and, as he enters, Thelma walks angrily out of the closet, thinking it is Patsy on the other side when it is Archie.

The sense of comic irony here allows for Thelma to react with embarrassment and angry frustration at this turn of events. Her careful coaching of Patsy results in her being in the embarrassing position, while Patsy greets the man just fine. Still, Patsy smells a phony and responds sarcastically to his conversation:

THELMA: Tell me about your travels.
ARCHIE: The last time, I was away for five years.
PATSY: Did you get time off for good behavior?
ARCHIE: In England, you can live off a guinea a week.
PATSY: Here too, if she's working

Left to right: Benny Baker, Patsy Kelly, Thelma Todd and Eddie Phillips in *Three Chumps Ahead* **(1934).**

Thelma corners Patsy in the kitchen, away from Archie, and tells her to behave, and to prepare some food. This is performed comedically. Thelma ushers Patsy into the kitchen and closes the door behind them. All we hear are loud noises as the camera stays focused on Archie in the living room, and then it cuts to Thelma practically pushing Patsy over in the kitchen, yelling at her to behave. Patsy continues to insist that Archie is a phony, but agrees to make some sandwiches.

In another of the funnier moments in the film, Patsy chooses to prepare limburger cheese sandwiches. This allows Thelma and Archie to react to the smell, Thelma fuming with anger and exhibiting that in her very funny facial expressions. Archie is discernibly turned off. In fact, one of the best laughs in the movie is when Patsy first brings out the tray of sandwiches, and quickly opens a window to ventilate the area.

The film's rhythm accelerates further when Archie phones his crude sailor brother Benny and tells him to come over and connect with Patsy. He does, and soon he is preoccupied with eating a limburger sandwich and singing loudly and off-key as Patsy plays the piano. Archie sneaks Thelma out to a nightclub. Benny was in on this ruse; Patsy drags him into the kitchen and beats him up until he tells her where the others have gone.

Director Gus Meins wisely realizes that the confrontation between Patsy and Benny would be funnier off-screen. She drags the much larger man into the kitchen and asks him once more when Archie and Thelma went. "I won't tell," he yells. After that we hear a lot of violent noise as the scene cuts to the nightclub where Archie and Thelma are cavorting. When they look up, they see slipper-clad Patsy accompanied by Benny, who has a black eye. The visual works perfectly. Meins first shoots Patsy's familiar slippers and then pans up to show a disgruntled Benny sitting beside her.

At this point, the film appears to have been influenced by a couple of earlier Laurel and Hardy comedies, *Men O' War* (1929) and *Below Zero* (1930). In the former, the boys have only 15 cents and want to buy a couple of sodas for two girls. Laurel is instructed to state that he doesn't want anything, and can't get the hang of it. In the latter, the duo finds a wallet, invites a cop to dinner, and discovers the wallet belongs to the cop.

The same general concept is utilized for the conclusion of this short. Archie is quite obviously low on funds, and Benny has no money at all. It is also discovered that anyone who cannot pay their bill is roughed up by a hulking maître d' and his waiter cohorts. Patsy, taking all of this in, orders nearly everything on the menu, hoping Archie's fate will be the same. Instead, Archie indicates he is going to charge their dinner, and goes to speak to the hostess, instructing that Patsy and Thelma nod to him on cue. They do so, but what Archie says to the hostess is that the women are going to pay for everything. He leaves the restaurant, and the final shot shows Thelma and Patsy in the back washing a mountainous amount of dishes.

While *Variety* dismissed *Three Chumps Ahead* as "a fairish sort of comedy [that] won't send the customers into ecstasy,"[7] it's actually quite funny and allows the girls to further define their relationship. Patsy has become the cynical protector of her more romantic and naïve friend, coming off as much more of a leader than ZaSu had been in the earlier films. *Variety* also stated, "Thelma Todd furnishes the looks, and Patsy Kelly the laughs." While she is quite attractive, Thelma was also very funny in her reactive behavior to her boisterous pal. The fact that Patsy is noisier does not mean that Thelma is any less funny.

Variety continued, "These two size up as a swell team and when they're good enough to overcome the handicap of such trite material, they're plenty good." Curiously, this film is somewhat more detailed than a lot of their other movies. Thelma and Patsy work from their established characters, while actors Eddie Phillips and Benny Baker, playing Archie and Benny, respectively, play supporting roles that bolster the proceedings nicely. They are the male counterparts, and get the last laugh. While this may not be particularly gratifying for viewers, it is funnier.

One-Horse Farmers (1934)

Directed by Gus Meins; *Produced by* Hal Roach; *Cinematographer:* Francis Corby; *Editor:* Bert Jordan; *Cast:* Thelma Todd, Patsy Kelly, James C. Morton, Billy Bletcher, Nora Cecil, Charlie Hall, Jack "Tiny" Lipson, Baldwin Cooke, Alex Novinsky, Fred Holmes; *Released by* MGM on August 1, 1934; Two Reels

One-Horse Farmers is a funny, fascinating comedy in which Thelma and Patsy attempt to leave their immediate surroundings and discover something easier and more fulfilling. This has become something of a common theme in their two-reelers, and *One-Horse Farmers* takes this idea to another level.

Tired of the hustle-bustle of city life, the girls are duped into buying their own farm where they can escape into a life of tranquil solitude. When they arrive at the property, they discover a shack surrounded by sand where it would be impossible to keep livestock or grow crops. The film then responds to this situation with a series of comic ideas.

One-Horse Farmers begins immediately with a creative establishing shot of a tin of sardines, then fades into a crowded subway. It is so crowded that when Patsy reaches back to scratch an itch, she ends up groping an old lady. It is here that a sharp operator sells Patsy the farm, which he calls Paradise Acres. Thelma is immediately against the idea. This is an interesting difference

Poster for *One-Horse Farmers* (1934).

from the previous film *Three Chumps Ahead* where Patsy is the more reasonable one while Thelma is conned. The con in that film was about romance, something that could distract Thelma from her good senses. This time it is for a better life, something both girls seek, but Patsy is more impulsive and impractical.

The set-up is only seconds long, but expertly filmed. Perhaps director Gus Meins had the idea to open with the can of sardines as an establishing visual and the cutting into the crowded subway car where movement is impossible. The con man distracts Patsy at the perfect time. Everything about her and Thelma's life is stressful, even their transportation to and from a job they don't enjoy. Patsy removes herself from all manner of practicality. She does not stop and think about how difficult it would be for two city women to adapt to the life of farming, with its early hours and long days of hard work. She only considers the seclusion, growing their own food, responding to the leisure activity of the country at a more relaxed pace.

As the transition takes place, Meins offers another nice shot of the women driving to the farm, with livestock in their vehicle (including a goat and a cow). This funny visual is built upon when a duck gets caught in Thelma's hair, and the goat eats her new hat. This shows how difficult it will be for these city girls to deal with the unpredictability of the farm animals with which they will have to deal in their new situation.

When they arrive at the property and see it is nothing but sand, Thelma switches to a sarcastic mode just as Patsy might have if one of Thelma's ideas turned out to be short-sighted. Thelma pulls a dead tree out of the sand and repeats a line from the sales pitch: "Fresh fruit from our own orchard!" Meins punctuates this visual of vast waste surrounding a tattered shack by showing that one of the items the girls have brought is a lawn mower.

Punctuating visual humor continues when it is shown that the sand extends to inside the house. Building even further upon this visual, Thelma sits down and pours even more sand out of her shoe.

The comedy continues to be effectively expanded when a dust storm causes Patsy to bring some piglets into the house to protect them. They become a noisy problem while the girls try to prepare something to eat. Thelma bites into a sandwich and gets a mouthful of crunchy sand. Patsy tries to empty a sand-filled stove pipe and ends up pouring its sandy contents into Thelma's lap. When the wind picks up, a sandstorm rages, and neighbors who have lost their home seek refuge with Thelma and Patsy. This situation builds until the house becomes more crowded than the subway had been. As

Thelma and Patsy prepare for rustic life in *One-Horse Farmers* (1934).

the storm dies down, Thelma and Patsy seek refuge by climbing onto the roof. Meins brings the camera back to a long shot that shows the house practically buried by sand.

One-Horse Farmers has a good premise, a lot of strong visual shots, and examines the girls' relationship more deeply by showing that aspects of their personalities are interchangeable. Either can play the more reasoned reaction to the situation, the sarcastic cynic or the idealistic dreamer. For instance, in

I'll Be Suing You, Thelma goes along with a scheme while Patsy protests. In this film, Patsy goes along with a scheme while Thelma protests. So the formula has become a conning third party causing one of the girls to heed the misguided advice while the other rebels against it. *One-Horse Farmers* is among Thelma and Patsy's best comedies, and could also be considered one of the best Gus Meins–directed films as well. The premise allows for a lot of interesting visual ideas, and Meins uses the vast bleakness of the sand and the shack as a perfect extreme from the noisy, cramped, crowded subway.

Unfortunately, Meins was removed from this series after this short. His background directing the Buster Brown kid comedies in the silent era made him a more comfortable fit with the Our Gang comedies. Having already directed some of their standout films, Meins was told by Roach to concentrate exclusively on that series. The formula was set, Thelma and Patsy understood their characters, and there were other strong directors on the Roach lot. But Meins' contribution to this series was truly beneficial to the success of the two-reelers.

Thelma and Patsy escape to the roof in *One-Horse Farmers* (1934).

After the release of *One-Horse Farmers*, Thelma Todd starred opposite Jack LaRue in the low budget feature *Take the Stand*, which was based on a story by Earl Derr Biggers, creator of Charlie Chan, and directed by Phil Rosen, who went on to helm several Chan movies in the 1940s. This story of a radio announcer who is murdered by gangsters also featured Gail Patrick, Russell Hopton, Vince Barnett and Berton Churchill. Meanwhile, Patsy followed *One-Horse Farmers* with a supporting role in MGM's *The Girl from Missouri* with Jean Harlow, Lionel Barrymore, Franchot Tone, and Lewis Stone. Patsy also took a smaller supporting role in the Columbia release *The Party's Over.*

While she enjoyed doing the comedies with Patsy, Thelma was growing restless in the same manner as ZaSu Pitts had. Thelma took notice of fellow blonde film actresses like Jean Harlow and Carole Lombard truly growing in prestigious films, and Thelma's biggest fame came from two-reelers. While they have lived on and garnered great respect from film buffs, short comedies were not as well regarded in the industry in the 1930s. And while Thelma was contracted with RKO and received steady work from that studio, her appearances were mostly in support. The Wheeler and Woolsey feature *Cock-eyed Cavaliers* is today considered a very funny and outrageously clever costume comedy, but it didn't always click with audiences at the time of its initial release. Some theater owners complained of audience members walking out on it.

However, unlike ZaSu Pitts, Thelma was not interested in leaving Roach's employ. She enjoyed the comedies and was pleased with their success. She just wanted to achieve some success beyond those parameters, and often wished she could score a good role in a strong dramatic film like Jean Harlow did so consistently at MGM.

According to Michelle Morgan's book *The Ice Cream Blonde*, Todd's former director Roland West purchased a café that he wanted Thelma to manage. Thelma long desired to get involved in an activity outside of the movie business, and in the summer of 1934 she began managing Thelma Todd's Sidewalk Café. Visitors from all over the country were quite thrilled to be greeted by Thelma Todd at her café. Thelma delighted in meeting her fans, signing menus for them, even sitting and chatting at their table as they enjoyed dessert or coffee after the meal. It became something of an outlet that assisted Thelma's self-esteem.

When Thelma and Patsy returned to the Roach lot after working on their outside projects, they discovered that Gus Meins was no longer their director, and they were assigned James Parrott. Parrott was a top-flight director, and truly understood comedy. Despite losing Meins, the future for the series looked good.

Opened by Mistake (1934)

Directed by James Parrott; *Produced by* Hal Roach; *Cinematographer:* Art Lloyd; *Editor:* Louis McManus; *Cast:* Thelma Todd, Patsy Kelly, Nora Cecil, William Burress, Charles McAvoy, Allan Cavan, Fanny Cossar, James Eagles, Mary Egan, Charlie Hall, Robert McKenzie, Rose Plumer, Ronald Rondell, Betty Danko; *Released by* MGM on October 6, 1934; Two Reels

James Parrott, the replacement for Gus Meins, directed *Opened by Mistake*. There are more medium shots and close-ups, the camera holds on scenes longer to record reactions and slow burns, and there are scenes where the central object in the frame is in motion and is framed by the stillness of negative space. Parrott's cinematic technique responds well to the comedy, which is brilliantly staged, resulting in another one of Thelma and Patsy's finest two-reelers.

Parrott was known for being able to direct films in a collaborative manner, having helmed several films featuring his real-life older brother Charley Chase, as well as those featuring Laurel and Hardy. Chase, a veteran director himself, easily collaborated with Parrott, resulting in some of the comedian's best work. Laurel and Hardy films were usually supervised by Stan Laurel, so having a director who sought input from the leading players was beneficial to Laurel's vision as both a comedian and a filmmaker. In fact, Patsy Kelly told Leonard Maltin that Laurel would sometimes visit the set of one of her and Thelma Todd's movies and offer a suggestion that "would make the entire scene." Todd and Kelly might offer occasional suggestions, but they did not aspire to be filmmakers like Chase and Laurel were. Thus, Parrott's approach to their films would center on his own ideas for crafting the comedy that would be enhanced by the performances of his stars.

There is a certain extra significance to Parrott's success directing these comedies at this time. He was a very skilled comedian in silent comedies (sometimes incorrectly billed as his brother Charley Chase in later reissues of these movies). Films like *Shoot Straight* and *Dear Old Pal* (both 1923) are minor classics. He often directed his own subjects, as well as those featuring his brother, and the solo films of Stan Laurel. He successfully transitioned to talkies, continuing to direct Charley Chase and Laurel and Hardy comedies. As the mid–1930s approached, Parrott's excesses with drugs and alcohol were taking their toll, and his work was often spotty. But his work with Todd and Kelly was consistently quite good.

Opened by Mistake begins with Patsy as a lazy, ineffective operator at a business where her boss is frantically trying to get in touch with his broker. Patsy is shown disregarding incoming and outgoing calls as distractions from the crossword puzzle she is doing. Her disregard for responsibility extends to calling busy hospital nurse Thelma to obtain a crossword puzzle answer. Patsy, of course, gets fired.

The significance of this opening scene reminds us that this film was made during the Great Depression when businesses were faltering and the importance of selling at the right time could be life-or-death. Thus, the importance of the businessman getting in contact with his broker was understood by period moviegoers. They responded to the impact. It is played for comedy

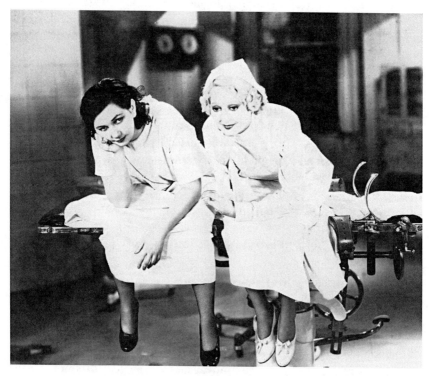

Patsy Kelly and Thelma Todd in *Opened by Mistake* (1934).

and used as a set-up, and is most effective in identifying Patsy as a gold-bricker.

With nowhere to go, she ends up at the window of the hospital where Thelma works. Fuming, Thelma must let Patsy in as it is pouring rain. To conceal her, Thelma sticks Patsy in an empty hospital room, but it turns out to be one where an emergency appendectomy patient is expected. Naturally Patsy is mistaken for that patient and must battle those who attempt to perform the surgery.

This is essentially the entire premise of *Opened by Mistake*, and the film builds upon it with a series of comic situations. Parrott effectively uses movement within the center of the frame which is surrounded by stillness as Patsy flails about while a doctor tries to take her pulse. A persnickety head nurse. engages in roughhouse slapstick with Patsy and they wrestle about. Nora Cecil, who plays the nurse, excelled in portraying thin-lipped, prune-faced schoolmarms and town gossips. This part is uncharacteristic of her usual performances. Her slapstick antics with Patsy allow her to be uninhibited.

In one of the better sequences, Patsy appears at the window trying to convince Thelma to let her stay. First, Thelma thinks someone is knocking at the door, but it turns out to be the window, and she opens the curtain to see Patsy leaning on the window, in the pouring rain, staring at her. Parrott holds on this scene for a while before Patsy is finally allowed in, making it even funnier. And Thelma doesn't cave to Patsy immediately, which adds a lot to the strength of her character in this film. At one point, as Patsy is climbing back out the window, she calls her back in, seemingly to let her stay, but it is actually just to give her an umbrella.

There are a couple of gags that can be attributed to the director's choice of presentation. When Thelma and Patsy first approach the vacant hospital room, Thelma shoves Patsy in and a crash is heard. When Thelma enters to see what happened, she finds Patsy entangled in a hospital tray cart and covered with dishes. We do not see the impact, we only hear the sound and are shown the results. This happens again when Thelma is shoved off camera. The resulting audial crash is followed by a shot of her lying on the floor, her head against the wall, and a fallen radio perched upon it. In each of these sequences, seeing the results after the sound of a crash, without showing the crash itself, is the director's idea for greater comic impact.

Another way of using this concept occurs when Patsy violently protests being wheeled on a stretcher into the operating room. She struggles violently against orderly Charlie Hall and nurse Nora Cecil. The picture then cuts to them having restrained Patsy while pushing the stretcher toward the operating room. Charlie has a black eye, and Nora is bruised with her hair mussed. The results are again presented without seeing the impact. It is a concept that works in each situation.

The director expands the battle between Patsy and the nurse. At one point, Nora and Patsy's wrestling causes Patsy to go flying out the window. This is quite similar to the 1932 Laurel and Hardy two-reeler *County Hospital,* when doctor Billy Gilbert tumbles out an upper floor window (in fact, it appears the same stock long shot is used here).

The fight concludes with the two of them fighting over an oxygen machine, with both Patsy and Nurse Nora trying to use it to knock out the other. They both get enough of a dose where their battle continues in sluggish slow motion. Already a funny visual, it is highlighted by a neat shot where Patsy jumps off the operating table onto Nora, knocking her to the floor, all done in slow motion. The idea of using slow motion makes their movements simultaneously graceful and ridiculous. It gives everything a dance-like quality, especially at one point when Thelma sees Patsy spinning in slow motion at the end of the hallway.

Opened by Mistake concludes with Thelma and Patsy escaping the hospital. Thelma appears to be escorting patient Patsy out on a stretcher. Instead, Patsy is walking out covered in cloth with two crutches held out to simulate feet. There is some slapstick when they walk into a traffic jam and a cop ends up going down a manhole, but the film ends triumphantly with a happy Thelma and Patsy walking off arm in arm.

There are a lot of layers to *Opened by Mistake.* The series retains its formula where Patsy is the cut-up who gets into trouble, and Thelma is the more responsible character who tries to retain balance and fumes at the problems her partner causes. It does not explore their relationship as that has now been fully established and examined with previous films.

The new director instead explores the comic possibilities of the characters and their situations. Parrott, despite off-screen excesses that impeded his success, was a very perceptive comedy director. His camera placement, choice of shots, and comic ideas effectively enhanced every Roach movie he helmed. Because neither Thelma nor Patsy were filmmakers, *Opened by Mistake* is purely his comic vision, and they respond beautifully. It is a film of outrageous situations, wild slapstick and a triumphant ending. There is no real plot or conclusion, but there is an effective comic structure.

Opened by Mistake was a big hit. Exhibitors reported to the trades almost unanimously that their patrons responded to this short as perhaps the best Todd–Kelly comedy to date. This is not to undermine Gus Meins' successful work with these comedies. He was responsible for the building up of the series' success as far back as when ZaSu Pitts was still actively partnered with Thelma. But Hal Roach felt that his talents were best served with the Our Gang comedies, and that became his chief focus. Meins would randomly return to the series.

After the release of *Opened by Mistake*, Patsy went to RKO for a small role in the feature *Transatlantic Merry-Go-Round* with Gene Raymond and Jack Benny.

Done in Oil (1934)

Directed by Gus Meins; *Produced by* Hal Roach; *Cinematographer:* Francis Corby; *Editor:* Roy Snyder; *Cast:* Thelma Todd, Patsy Kelly, Arthur Housman, Eddie Conrad, Leo White, Art Rowlands, Rolfe Sedan, William Wagner; *Released by* MGM on November 10, 1934; Two Reels

Filmed in the summer of 1934, *Done in Oil* was probably shot before *Opened by Mistake* because Gus Meins is directing. As indicated in the previous chapters, Meins was considered most effective helming the Our Gang comedies. James Parrott had brought a different perspective to *Opened by Mistake* and now *Done in Oil* is somewhat more akin to the standard method of presentation. This is not a negative. Meins was a great director for this series, having developed an effective formula, and he helped with the transition from ZaSu Pitts to Patsy Kelly.

Done in Oil is a fun look at artistic expression. Because Patsy and Thelma are always low on money and attempting to better their station (even in those films where one or both are gainfully employed), it is a good idea for them to be involved in the art world. The "starving artist" idea suits their formula. And the idea that some oddball art lovers are responding to their work is a solid comic development.

Done in Oil opens with Thelma carefully painting while Patsy models, wearing a wig. Patsy complains that her back hurts and that she is hungry. "Michelangelo did some of his best work while broke," says Thelma. "This place should be filled with masterpieces," Patsy responds.

Meins uses a lot of tracking shots in the opening scenes; there are paintings and drawings hung all about, so many that Thelma has trouble finding room for her latest work. All of these art pieces occupying the negative space gives a deeper level to the visuals, without being cluttered. It is actually quite artful itself.

The conflict is presented in standard fashion: a cranky landlord demanding back rent, then concluding his scene by tripping on the carpet sweeper and doing a wild pratfall. The brainstorm to acquire some money comes from a drunken friend (Arthur Housman) who rechristens Thelma "Madame La Todd," while Patsy will be her maid, Fifi. From this set-up, the usual formula of Thelma desperately trying to pull off the ruse while Patsy's natural boorishness threatens to ruin everything is utilized via a trio of French art lovers who will (the girls hope) buy some paintings.

The fact that the drunk is the one who dreamed up this whole scene is rather amusing. There is a funny bit where he goes to take a picture of Thelma, but finds that he had put an empty glass in his camera. His response: "Oops, wrong lens!"

Eddie Conrad, Rolfe Sedan and Leo White camp it up as the French art patrons who cavort about the house looking at the paintings, with florid reactions (presented by Meins in tight close-ups) while Thelma and Patsy try hard to make them comfortable. When Patsy is introduced as a French maid, the art lovers are delighted and start conversing with her in French. But all Patsy can do is respond "oui oui" and with no French accent at all.

As with many comedies from this era, politically incorrect racial humor shows up in a scene where the drunk friend Arthur shows up with food for the patrons. Thelma wants to make it seem that the food was cooked on site, so Patsy (as Fifi) is asked to go get the cook, Magnolia. Patsy goes into the kitchen and comes out in blackface, wearing stereotypical mammy clothing. She camps it up, dancing around and saying "Yassah boss" in order to make the ruse work.

A scene like this seems quite unsettling in today's more enlightened era, and it is easy to explain it away by indicating that this is a comedy, and no real harm was intended. And the scene has a historical context. But we no longer laugh at such a scene. We respond with an appalled fascination that such ideas passed as innocent comic satire when this movie was shot in 1934.

The film concludes with a fun twist. Patsy goes into the kitchen, takes off the blackface and changes clothes. She imbibes with Arthur and starts painting on a blank canvas. It's nothing more than random brush strokes, but naturally the Frenchmen want it and start a bidding war with Arthur, who insists Patsy painted it for him. The bidding reaches $1500 (nearly $30,000 in

Patsy Kelly and Thelma Todd enter the art world in *Done in Oil* (1934).

21st century money). However, it is discovered that Patsy has backed into the painting, causing it to leave the canvas and end up on the backside of her skirt.

Done in Oil is not a bad short, but it is a bit noisier and more haphazard than the previous *Opened by Mistake*. In fact, as James Parrott took over the direction for four shorts, he continued to bring a stronger comic dynamic to the films that he had honed since the silent era. *Done in Oil* was super-bizarre, even surreal at times. For instance, there is a scene where all the Frenchmen are laughing hysterically. The camera cuts between close-ups of all their faces as they laugh, making the scene feel very dizzy and strange. And the blackface scene takes up so much of the film, it distracts from the rest of it.

When *Done in Oil* hit theaters, the trades were reasonably impressed. *The Motion Picture Herald* stated, "The attractive Thelma Todd and the plump Patsy Kelly combine their efforts in this comedy to achieve a result which is, for the most part, a fair comedy."[8] *Motion Picture Daily* called it "an amusing short. Miss Todd and particularly Miss Kelly resort less to slapstick here than in any of their previous comedies and the results are much more favorable. The dialogue is appropriate and the situations and entire story are novel."[9] *Film Daily* called *Done in Oil* "[g]ood slapstick," adding, "Miss Kelly supplies most of the laughs."[10]

About a month after the release of *Done in Oil*, Thelma was seen in the RKO feature *Lightning Strikes Twice*, featuring Ben Lyon and Pert Kelton (who would soon figure prominently in the Roach two-reelers). While it was produced as a farce, Thelma approached *Lightning Strikes Twice* as a drama, and it allowed her to expand her work as an actress. *Lightning Strikes Twice* is one of her best films and features one of her finest performances. And the film is filled with such actors as Laura Hope Crews, Skeets Gallagher, Chick Chandler, Walter Catlett, Jonathan Hale, Fred Kelsey and Edgar Dearing, some of whom Thelma had worked with before.

Thelma also continued her work at her Sidewalk Café, and when she'd be seen dining with Roland West, they could indicate to gossip mongers that they were simply talking business, not rekindling their romance. Thelma was always bothered by her personal life becoming gossip tabloid fodder, and wished more attention would be given her screen work.

According to Michelle Morgan in *The Ice Cream Blonde*, things were not always running smoothly at the café, one such problem almost seeming like a routine out of a Roach comedy.[11]

Customers at the café were greeted by an eclectic menu.... However, if they dared complain about the food they were served, there was trouble in the kitchen. The Viennese chef enjoyed inventing new, creative ways of serving food but was not so good at accepting criticism. If anyone dared complain that his steaks were undercooked, he'd stamp on the meat with his foot, sling it back into the fire, and then—unknown to Thelma—serve it up again to the unsuspecting customer.

Bum Voyage (1934)

Directed by Nick Grinde; *Produced by* Hal Roach; *Cinematographer:* Ernest Depew; *Editor:* Louis McManus; *Cast:* Thelma Todd, Patsy Kelly, Adrian Rosley, Noah Young, Germaine De Neel, Francis Sayles, Constant Frank, Charles Gemora, Sydney Jarvis, Florence Wix, Albert Petit, Marie Wilson; *Released by* MGM on December 15, 1934; Two Reels

By this, their thirteenth comedy together, Thelma and Patsy had their formula and their performance down to an exact science. The premise and gag situations are pretty typical, but the performances are first-rate.

Thelma and Patsy, once again down on their luck financially, get kicked out of their apartment on a cold night. In another apartment, a French performer, Madame Zaza, tells her manager that she no longer wants to perform with the trained gorilla that is part of her act. Refusing to attend her next gig, she angrily tosses two steamer tickets out the window. Thelma and Patsy find them and decide to "bum" a voyage off someone else's fare.

This is a comfortable set-up for the film, as it is so similar a premise to the duo's previous efforts. Again they are out of money. Again they don't know what to do or where to go. And again fortune falls into their laps, but there are catches. First, the tickets are not their property. They will have to assume the identity of others. But the biggest catch is discovered once they arrive at the ship and Thelma claims to be Madame Zaza and Patsy her assistant. The gorilla has preceded them and is waiting, caged, in their stateroom.

This is the start of the comic conflict, and director Nick Grinde sets it up nicely. The accommodations are impressive, they are surrounded by opulence, and then they see the gorilla for which they are now responsible. The other problem is that Thelma, being Zaza, is a hired performer who is expected to do her act for the other passengers, and this means she must perform with the gorilla. Patsy finds a gorilla suit costume among the effects, and the plan is that Patsy will don the gorilla suit and perform with Thelma. The audience will be so primed to be entertained, that the girls can simply ad-lib an act of any sort and it will pacify all involved.

Predictably, the gorilla escapes, and it is up to Thelma and Patsy to recapture and cage it. There are some obvious mechanical gags (Patsy running on a treadmill and getting nowhere with the gorilla in pursuit), while in other cases the premise allows for expanding to some more clever material. A mirror scene between Patsy (in the gorilla suit) and the actual gorilla is a highlight. Groucho and Harpo Marx had performed perhaps the best version of this comic sequence in their 1933 feature *Duck Soup* (Harpo would later do the same scene with Lucille Ball on a noted 1955 episode of *I Love Lucy*). Patsy and Charles Gemora, who plays the gorilla, perform their own mirror scene quite effectively.

The film moves toward its conclusion when Thelma gets prepared to do the act with Patsy in costume, not realizing it is the real gorilla who has bounded on stage. Thelma continually scolds the animal for its disruption, thinking she is merely redirecting her friend. The captain of the ship ends up wrestling with the real gorilla. Thelma gets to be involved in some really good physical comedy in these scenes, such as one instance where the gorilla pushes her across the room and she crashes through a drum.

The final shot is surreal. It shows Thelma, Patsy and the gorilla floating along in a lifeboat and hitchhiking with their thumbs out as ships pass by. The back projection looks pretty poor (even for 1934) but the concept is still funny. It is reminiscent of another Hal Roach production, the Laurel and Hardy feature *Sons of the Desert*, in which Stan and Ollie tell their wives they "ship-hiked" home after a ship they were supposed to be on sank.

A master at playing apes of all kinds, Charles Gemora frequently showed up in Roach films. He played the title role in *The Chimp* with Laurel and Hardy and the gorilla in that duo's feature film *Swiss Miss* (Patsy Kelly called this her favorite Laurel and Hardy movie). He also was in *At the Circus* with the Marx Brothers, *So This Is Africa* with Wheeler and Woolsey, *Road to Zanzibar* and *Road to Morocco* with Bob Hope and Bing Crosby, *Africa Screams* with Abbott and Costello, and *Nature in the Wrong* with Charley Chase. Not limited to comedies, Gemora played apes and ape-like creatures in *Island of Lost Souls, Murders in the Rue Morgue, Charlie Chan at the Circus*

Lobby card for *Bum Voyage* (1934).

114

and *Blonde Venus*. He had appeared with Thelma and ZaSu Pitts in *Sealskins* a few years earlier.

Canadian-born actress Germaine De Neel, who plays Madame Zaza, was the female lead in the French versions of Roach comedies. Hal Roach would re-film a lot of his comedies in other languages, casting the stars of the film with other actors who spoke the language (while the stars did their lines phonetically). De Neel co-starred in the French film *Les carottiers*, which combined the Laurel and Hardy shorts *Laughing Gravy* and *Be Big* into a longer subject. She had appeared with Thelma and ZaSu in *Red Noses* and *Pajama Party*.

Bum Voyage had a story that was pretty predictable, but entertaining in the way it is told. *Variety* said, "Nick Grinde, the director, has built a far above par comedy out of an ordinary story.... Story is a long way from new, but its telling is aces."[12] *Film Daily* called it a "good comedy" with "enough excitement and laughs to satisfy the crowds."[13]

Treasure Blues (1935)

Directed by James Parrott; *Produced by* Hal Roach; *Cinematographer:* Art Lloyd; *Editor:* William H. Terhune; *Cast:* Thelma Todd, Patsy Kelly, Arthur Housman, Sam Adams, Charlie Hall, Jack "Tiny" Lipson, James Finlayson [seen in a photograph]; *Released by* MGM on January 26, 1935; Two Reels

Filmed in the fall of 1934, *Treasure Blues* is the first of the Todd–Kelly shorts released in 1935, Thelma's final year of life. As 1935 began, her marriage to Pat De Cicco had ended and she was once again connected to filmmaker Roland West.

Patsy, meanwhile, became involved in a dispute regarding fellow Roach comics Stan Laurel and Oliver Hardy. In March of 1935,the trades announced that Laurel asked to be let out of his contract, leaving Hardy at Roach without his partner. Laurel indicated his request for more money and greater creative freedom were not accepted by the producer. Roach told the press that Laurel was unable to find suitable story material for himself and his partner (due mostly to conflicts Roach and Laurel had on the filming of *Babes in Toyland* in 1934). Trade announcements further stated that with Laurel gone, Roach planned to use Hardy in a series called The Hardys, featuring Patsy Kelly as his wife and Spanky McFarland as their mischievous son. Patsy told the author in 1976, "This was just an idea Roach had. We never shot anything. I kept working in the pictures with Thelma, and Laurel and Hardy ironed out their differences."

Laurel's conflict was not with Hardy, but with the producer. He eventually got what he wanted, producing features like *Our Relations* and *Way Out West* for his own company within the unit. The idea for The Hardys is intriguing, but it was likely a bargaining ploy by Roach. Ending the Todd–Kelly series and removing Spanky from the popular Our Gang films would not have been in his best interests. Thelma and Patsy were comfortably established in their comedies, and remained popular with critics and moviegoers. Patsy told interviewer Dena Reed in *Screenland* magazine:

> I just play myself. We all have a certain way of walking and certain gestures that make up our personality and distinguish us like our handwriting. That mine happen to be funny is just dandy for my pocketbook. When Thelma Todd and I have to look at our rushes in the projection room, we get hysterical—not because we think we're so good, but because we've had such a good time shooting the picture and it even got to the point where either of us had only to crook a finger to send the other into giggles for no earthly reason.[14]

In the same interview, Patsy recalled ZaSu Pitts: "I think she's the greatest comedienne on the screen today. I hate it when the papers say I was signed to take her place opposite Thelma. No one could ever fill her place." Patsy had by now, of course, made her own place in the comedies with Thelma Todd, and was doing some of her best work.

Treasure Blues again shows Thelma and Patsy as low on funds when they get a sudden windfall. This time, Patsy's uncle has died and left her his fortune, but it is at the bottom of the ocean. So the girls, and a drunken accomplice, go out in a boat with the intention of searching for it. After a series of mishaps, they finally discover the treasure by accident.

From this premise, *Treasure Blues* offers a lot of wild slapstick gags and remains outrageous and funny throughout. Director James Parrott is back, and his expertise at presenting comic visuals is what makes *Treasure Blues* so amusing. The first great visual occurs when Patsy's uncle's trunk arrives. She opens it and finds a diving outfit with her uncle's picture placed prominently at the head. It is a freak image that causes her to react big. The photo is of Roach favorite James Finlayson, making the comic visual striking in its familiarity to the viewer as well.

When Thelma returns home from work, she finds Patsy practicing in the bathtub wearing the diving equipment. More slapstick ensues when Patsy is unable to remove the diving helmet. It is then that they see plumber Arthur Housman (doing his drunk act) and the circumstances lead to him joining the girls on their journey. (He claims, "In my younger days, I used to be an old sea captain.")

The underwater effects are pretty good for a 1935 two-reeler, and this adds to the humor as Patsy goes into the ocean and starts wrestling with a swordfish. Thelma and Arthur try to pump enough air to Patsy and end up inflating her diving suit, causing her to float up out of the water. Arthur agrees to take her place, and when he goes underwater he discovers gold—but it is Old Gold champagne. Delighted by his discovery, Arthur works hard to drink the liquor despite the underwater conditions. But the girls manage to pull the diving suit up and off of him as they bring him up from the deep. As they do, his foot get tangled onto the actual treasure chest, filled with riches, and it is brought into the boat. As the trio dances about in celebration, they knock the treasure back into the ocean. When this happens, they all dive into the water to retrieve it as the film ends.

Some of the slapstick in *Treasure Blues* is pretty wild during the sequence when they are trying to remove Patsy's diving helmet. At one point they stick her head in a vise and start pulling on her body. This is similar to a sequence in the later Three Stooges two-reeler *Higher Than a Kite*, in which Moe gets his head caught in a pipe and Larry and Curly attempt the same method to extricate him. For the Stooges, it works. Violent comedy was part of their established forte. It does not always work for Thelma and Patsy. In fact, Leonard Maltin in *The Great Movie Shorts* pointed out that the sort of rough slapstick performed by male comedians was not always as funny when it

Poster for *Treasure Blues* (1935).

117

happened to females. Here it seems a bit extreme. Still, overall, *Treasure Blues* has enough good comedy to sustain it.

Arthur Housman, often was relegated to bit parts, has one of his larger roles here. He was often very funny as the drunken accomplice, and when he gets a more extended part in films like *Scram* (1932) and *The Live Ghost* (1934) with Laurel and Hardy, or this Todd–Kelly comedy, he adds a good deal to the proceedings. He also had a nice bit in the 1936 Laurel and Hardy feature *Our Relations* and appeared in some Columbia shorts, notably with the Three Stooges and Andy Clyde. In fact, in the Three Stooges film *Punch Drunks* (1934), Housman plays a sober ring attendant at a boxing match. Perhaps his best non-drunk performance is in *Next Door Neighbor* (1930) in which he and Edgar Kennedy play neighbors at odds because while Arthur wants to take a nap, songwriter Edgar is loudly trying to compose a song on his clanky piano. It has been claimed in some studies that alcoholism was a problem Housman had in real life, and it hampered his career. However, the statistics seem to conflict with that claim. Housman remained active from the silent era until his death in 1942. He even had his own production company for a brief time during the 1920s. Also, Housman had a lasting and stable marriage to Ellen Grubley from 1919 until his passing 23 years later.

Film Daily called *Treasure Blues* a "good comedy," adding, "Helped in no small measure by Arthur Housman, this two-reel comedy packs plenty of laughs. It is also out of the rut from a production status."[15]

Sing Sister Sing (1935)

Directed by James Parrott; *Produced by* Hal Roach; *Cinematographer:* Art Lloyd; *Editor:* William H. Terhune; *Cast:* Thelma Todd, Patsy Kelly, Harry Bowen, Charlie Hall, Arthur Housman; *Released by* MGM on March 2, 1935; Two Reels

On February 25, 1935, only days before the release of the latest Todd–Kelly comedy *Sing Sister Sing*, Thelma received an anonymous note demanding that she pay $10,000 to Abe Lyman in New York, or she would die. The note was sent to her at the Hal Roach Studio, and it disrupted her personal life greatly. The police were called, and the information hit the newspapers by early March. Thelma was angered that some law officials wondered if it were merely a publicity stunt cooked up by the studio, when in fact her life really was in danger.

Lyman was a man Thelma had once dated. He was not involved in the writing of the letters; in fact, he was receiving them as well, expecting to collect the money from Thelma until further notice, when he would be contacted by the extortionists. Thelma was living alone at the time, in an apartment above her café. The letters, demands and threats continued for months, limiting both her social activities and her work in feature films outside of the Roach Studio. In June, she returned home to find that her apartment had been burglarized. It eventually got to the point where Thelma went to work in the Roach comedies and was escorted home immediately after filming, remaining there until the next day. On August 17, 1935, a building superintendent, Harry Schimanski, was arrested and charged with extortion. No more letters were received after his arrest, even after he was out on bail.

While *Sing Sister Sing* was released on March 2, 1935, it was shot before the initial February 25 extortion letter was received. One of the best and most unusual Todd–Kelly comedies, it examines the duo's relationship from another perspective. This time Thelma is the more difficult one, and Patsy is the put-upon one who reacts with slow burns. It is she who must keep Thelma out of trouble. Patsy is also in a position to measure up to Thelma's standards, while her friend is a haughty acquaintance, not a partner.

The film opens with Patsy coming to live with Thelma at a swanky hotel (Thelma needs a roommate to share expenses). When the girls meet, it is as if they had not seen each other in some time; they do not play an organic team like in their other films. Thelma extols the virtues of the hotel: "There are real sheets on the bed, all the hot water you want, and the air is just like wine." But shortly thereafter, she lists a rigid set of rules that Patsy must follow. One of the main ones: no quarreling. If either gets angry or frustrated, they are to start singing. That will defuse their anger.

From this point, Patsy must somehow fit into the lifestyle that Thelma has already created for herself. She is to have half of the closet, but Thelma's dresses crowd the entire area. The dresser is so jammed with Thelma's things, the clothes rise up when Patsy slides the drawers out. When Patsy tries to wash up before bed, Thelma goes through an entire ritual of cleaning, making up and affixing a chin strap, each time shoving Patsy out of the way. Patsy lies down to sleep in the double bed, and is told she is on Thelma's side. When Patsy turns out the light, Thelma screams and says she is afraid of the dark. To top it all off, Thelma starts sleepwalking and ends up out on the building ledge, high above the ground, and a frantic Patsy must retrieve her. She then ties a rope to Thelma's ankle and the other end to her own, as a precaution.

Thelma is awakened by an alarm, gets up and falls because of the rope fastened to her ankle. She then decides that this situation will not work, and Patsy has to move out.

Thelma and Patsy were sometimes referred to as "the female Laurel and Hardy," because Stan and Ollie set the foundation for comedy teams at that time, and were also working at Roach. *Sing Sister Sing* is quite close to the Laurel and Hardy dynamic, most especially regarding Patsy's reaction to the series of frustrations she endures throughout. Like Oliver Hardy, Patsy fumes with a slow burn and stares at nothing in particular in reaction to what Thelma does to inconvenience her. What makes this even more fascinating is that this is usually the role Thelma would play. The formula normally would have presented Patsy coming to the hotel and taking over, making a shambles of things, and Thelma fuming. This time it is the other way around, and Patsy rises to the occasion while Thelma very comfortably plays the quietly troublesome roommate.

Having Patsy continually sing to express her anger is very funny, and the role reversal makes sense because Thelma isn't obnoxious in the way that Patsy usually is. She is very haughty in the things she says and the way she talks. At one point Patsy says she only washes her face with soap and water and Thelma replies "Hmm, I thought so." It makes sense that the less posh Patsy would react to Thelma's demands the way she does.

There is a vignette where Patsy gathers Thelma's many different hats and tries them each on, having attained permission to choose one of them for herself. It is a reworking of a similar sequence from Buster Keaton's silent feature *Steamboat Bill Jr.* (1927), that would be used again by Curly Howard in the Three Stooges two-reeler *Three Dumb Clucks* (1937). Patsy tries on each hat, and none of them look very good on her. It is comical how each of them fit so absurdly. Rather than photograph Patsy head-on as if she were looking in a mirror, James Parrott chooses to place the camera behind Patsy and shoot her reflection. It is artfully done, and the *mise en scène* is much more effective. Patsy finally chooses a hat and goes to show Thelma.

PATSY: I like this one. If I take it, will you miss it?
THELMA: No, but the hotel might. That's a lamp shade

The scene where Thelma sleepwalks out onto the ledge is a good bit of frantic comedy. Patsy goes out and gets her foot tangled in the blinds drawstring. She crawls onto the ledge and watches in horror while Thelma walks onto the top of the hotel marquee. She manages to get into a window and pull the marquee toward her, so that Thelma walks into that same window, back to her room, and into bed, without having any idea of the danger she had faced or the trouble she caused. (An entire episode of TV's *The Honeymooners* used this same concept. It was also the basis for the Popeye cartoon *Dream Walking*.)

There are a few tangential slapstick moments, such as Patsy trying to control a noisy radiator, but accidentally turning on the emergency fire hose. The water pressure causes the hose to move about and spray water. Drunk Arthur Housman walks into the hallway, sees the hose, thinks it's a snake and runs away frightened.

The running gag throughout these frustrations is Patsy suddenly singing each time she is confronted by another maddening situation. They are relentless, they build upon each other, and the pace set by Parrott's competent direction maintains a good comic rhythm.

Film Daily called *Sing Sister Sing* a "satisfactory comedy [with] enough in it to provide a satisfying number of laughs."[16] It was well-received by moviegoers and remains one of Thelma and Patsy's most offbeat, effective and funniest comedies.

The Tin Man (1935)

Directed by James Parrott; *Produced by* Hal Roach; *Cinematographer:* Art Lloyd; *Editor:* Louis McManus; *Cast:* Thelma Todd, Patsy Kelly, Matthew Betz, Clarence Wilson, Cy Slocum, Billy Bletcher (voice only); *Released by* MGM on March 30, 1935; Two Reels

Despite the stress regarding the extortion letters that continued over several months, Thelma Todd tried to enjoy her successful life. In the press, she shared interesting recipes from her café, and invited photographers to visit the set of her movies with Patsy Kelly.

For her part, Patsy was now, on her 15th film with Thelma, finally settled into the idea of filmmaking. It was stated in a feature on Patsy by Julia Gwin for *Silver Screen* magazine:

> The first day [in movies] was like a nightmare—people shouting, electricians, cameramen, assistant directors chasing about hectically, until Patsy decided she must be in some kind of madhouse. Even today there is still an element of unreality about Hollywood for her. She used to spend hours learning her lines, but when she found that more often than otherwise the script was changed and written on the set as it was shot,

she decided there wasn't any use. "As for being in the actual 'take,'" she says, "it's slam-bam, rush every minute, and until I see the dailies I'm ever sure whether I'm just a stand-in or an actress."[17]

The same article indicates a quote from a young man the writer knew, a deaf mute: "All the deaf people love Patsy Kelly. She brings us a kind of comedy we can understand without words. She's like a female Charlie Chaplin." This compliment made Patsy very happy.

The Tin Man is a scare comedy like *Sealskins*, the haunted house short that Thelma did with ZaSu Pitts. And while it must again be emphasized that Gus Meins did a great job developing the successful formula that made this series work, James Parrott had a performer's background and a comic vision that enhanced the Roach comedies he helmed. This is immediately evident during the opening of *The Tin Man*: Thelma and Patsy are driving around trying to locate their destination. Patsy wrote down the address but used Thelma's pen.

THELMA: That pen hasn't had ink in it for months.
PATSY: Well, I wrote in the dark!

Just at that moment, the radio announces that Blackie, a dangerous criminal, has escaped from prison and is in the area. As this announcement concludes, a scary-looking man rises up in the back seat behind the girls. The escaped criminal has been hiding in their car.

Parrott shoots this scene head-on, with the girls surrounded by darkness, but spaced just enough apart in the foreground, allowing the menacing face of the criminal to rise up in the background. Patsy resumes driving just as the criminal is reaching up to grab both women. She drives over a rock, causing the escaped prisoner to hit his head and get knocked out. Both Thelma and Patsy remain completely oblivious to his presence.

The women are lost, and it starts raining, so they stop the car at a house that has its lights on and go to ask directions. When Patsy reaches in the back seat for an umbrella, Parrott shoots, in close-up, her hand hovering over the unconscious criminal, then grabbing the umbrella without touching him or realizing he is there.

The house is occupied by a mad scientist who has built a robot programmed to destroy all women. The man seeks vengeance against females for "ignoring, sniping and insulting me." From this point, the film balances between the girls attempting to deal with the scientist and the robot that he is controlling from another room, as well as Blackie's plight. He has awakened in the car and entered the house unobserved. He hides from the action, but is nearby.

The girls attempt to escape through a window, but each time they open one, another is under it. When they get to the end, they are frightened by a scary painting. The menacing robot enters and forces the girls to sit down at a table. He pulls a chair out from under Patsy, making her fall down. She does the same to the robot and he remains in the air. He tries to make them drink oil, and Patsy pours hers out under the table. This is where Blackie is hiding and it ends up being poured on him. More slapstick ensues, and it seems any time something is thrown or discarded, it hits Blackie who is hiding in various places nearby. He takes a beating throughout.

Patsy pours water on the robot, causing it to go haywire and attack the professor, chasing him out of the house. Thelma and Patsy run back to their car, and are met by Blackie, who is once again in the back seat. They scream,

Left to right: Patsy Kelly, Thelma Todd, Cy Slocum and Clarence Wilson in *The Tin Man* (1935).

but he quiets them and weeps, "I'm not going to hurt you, just please take me back to my nice quiet prison cell!"

There are some good ideas in *The Tin Man* and some nice visuals from the creative director. Unfortunately, nothing is particularly scary, and the comedy is not terribly inspired. Clarence Wilson, who made a career out of playing crotchety old men opposite W.C. Fields, Charley Chase, Our Gang and others, is amusingly cast as the vengeful mad scientist. Cy Slocum, Oliver Hardy's stand-in and stunt man, plays the robot, but it is Billy Bletcher's deep voice we hear. The robot looks more comical than menacing, which appears to be the intention.

Matthew Betz is an interesting choice to play the escaped convict. A 20-year veteran of film by this time, Betz had pretty quickly carved a niche in bad guy roles, but didn't do a lot with comedy. He was in such noted silents as *Burn 'Em Up Barnes* (1921) with Johnny Hines, appeared in several Lon Chaney features, including the 1925 *The Unholy Three*, and had a supporting role in *The Patent Leather Kid* (1927) with Richard Barthelmess. In talkies, he had small roles in a few comedies such as *The Captain Hates the Sea* (1934) in which the Three Stooges also appear, and W.C. Fields' *Mississippi* (1935). Other than *The Tin Man*, Betz can be spotted in a couple of Buster Keaton sound shorts, *The E-Flat Man* and *Jail Bait*. He died in 1938.

Critics were pleased with *The Tin Man*. The review in *Film Daily* called it a "clever novelty. ... Matthew Betz as an escaped convict hiding in the house adds to the hilarity."[18] Theater owners stated that their patrons reacted to *The Tin Man* with hearty laughter.

A few days after this film's release, Thelma Todd appeared at a rodeo conducted by cowboy star Hoot Gibson. Others who appeared included Clark Gable, Bing Crosby and Clara Bow. Because of the continuing extortion letters, the number of Thelma's personal appearances dwindled.

The Misses Stooge (1935)

Directed by James Parrott; *Produced by* Hal Roach; *Cinematographer:* Walter Lundin; *Editor:* William Terhune; *Cast:* Thelma Todd, Patsy Kelly, Herman Bing, Esther Howard, Rafael Storm, Henry Rocquemore, Harry Bowen, William O'Brien, Dennis O'Keefe; *Released by* MGM on April 20, 1935; Two Reels

By the time Thelma and Patsy were making *The Misses Stooge,* Thelma's divorce from Pat De Cicco had become finalized. Furthermore, she was revealing to close friends that she was tiring of doing two-reel comedies and once again desired a good role in a more prestigious picture. Thus, it is amusing that *The Misses Stooge* features Thelma as a haughty performer who believes Patsy's earthiness is bringing her down. Thelma indicates that she operates in a higher sphere than her partner, and believes they should go their separate ways. However, they both end up working for the same magician, Patsy as his assistant and Thelma as his stooge.

The show biz word "stooge" has taken on different meanings over the years, especially since it is no longer in regular use. Ted Healy, an acquaintance of Thelma's, once had an act where he was the star and there were three minions on stage with him that he basically slapped around. They were his stooges. When the men who played these roles broke away from him and started a series of comedies at Columbia, they called themselves the Three Stooges. Moe Howard, Larry Fine, and Jerry (Curly) Howard were popular in their day, but constant TV revivals have caused them to achieve iconic status. Thus, the term "stooge" is usually identified with them.

In 1953, Paramount released a feature film starring Dean Martin and Jerry Lewis entitled *The Stooge*, in which Dean was an egotistical vaudeville performer who hired comical Jerry to stooge for him—to enhance his act by cutting up in the audience and eventually join him on stage.

In the context of this Todd–Kelly short, Thelma's being the stooge means that she is the one on whom the magician performs his tricks. She is levitated, she is made to disappear, etc. Patsy, as the assistant, remains on stage with the magician and assists with his performance.

Botching a magic act, having the tricks turn on the performer, has been done by a few different comedians: Buster Keaton in *Mixed Magic* (1936), Harold Lloyd in *Movie Crazy* (1932), and Curly Howard repeating the Lloyd bit in the Three Stooges short *Loco Boy Makes Good* (1941). In this Todd–Kelly comedy, this premise offers some creative comedy.

At one point, Thelma is levitated by the magician, but he is then knocked out on stage, leaving his stooge freely floating. Patsy panics as Thelma floats, like a balloon, out of the auditorium, then out of the hotel, ending up above the pool. Reaching out from a diving board, Patsy tries to bring her down. But a guard dog climbs onto the diving board and knocks Patsy into the pool. This sequence concludes with a soaked Patsy returning to the stage, pulling a floating Thelma with a rope as if she's a kite.

During a trick where Thelma disappears from a box, she leaves through a secret panel and is accosted by one of the society men, who flirts with her.

Holding her hand and not letting her go, Thelma is concerned that he will ruin the illusion. Patsy fires a bow and arrow (it's part of the act) and when the magician reveals what's in the box, he sees a man with an arrow sticking out of his backside, yowling away.

The film ends rather abruptly with a big gag: Thelma is once again in the clutches of a man, escapes, but falls into a cannon that is loaded up for the closing trick. The cannon turns and fires at the audience, as the picture fades from a billow of smoke to the end title.

The Misses Stooge explores show business but also examines the Thelma–Patsy screen relationship. Interestingly, when someone walks by early in the film and insults the girls, it is Thelma who is about to start a fight and Patsy who calms her down. Usually it is the other way around. Thelma calls upon the haughtiness she exhibited in *Sing Sister Sing*, just desserts when she ends up in the same act as Patsy, but subordinate to her.

German-born Herman Bing, who plays the magician, came to this country with F.W. Murnau and worked on Murnau's classic silent feature *Sunrise* (1927). He carved a niche in Hollywood features, playing comical German characters. Some of his better performances are found in *Footlight Parade* (1933) and *Call of the Wild* (1935). Bing did very little in short comedies. Before *The Misses Stooge*, he appeared in a Mack Sennett short entitled *The Plumber and the Lady* (1933) and a Clark and McCullough short called *Fits in a Fiddle*, and also was in an Educational Pictures short, *Trimmed in Furs* (1934). So Bing just dabbled in short films and concentrated more on small parts in features. His comic German accent works well in this film, entertaining the audience during the magic show with lines like "The last time I did this trick it was for the crowned heads of Europe. Then I came to America!"

Thelma Todd and Patsy Kelly in *The Misses Stooge* (1935).

It is also good to see Esther Howard in the role of a dowager. Later this same year, she appeared at Columbia with Andy Clyde in his comedy *It Always Happens* (1935), and co-starred with him frequently in his two-reelers for that studio. She didn't continue to work in Hal Roach productions, but did act with Laurel and Hardy in their later 20th Century–Fox feature *The Big Noise* (1944). Howard had an extensive career in films, comedies and dramas, features and shorts, working frequently with director Preston Sturges, and making an impact in the drama *Murder, My Sweet* (1944).

The effects enhance the comedy in *The Misses Stooge*. The bit with Thelma levitated and Patsy trying to rescue her is quite well done for 1935 when special effects were more technologically limited. And the shot of a wet, angry Patsy stomping back on stage pulling a floating Thelma on a rope is a great comic visual. The only weak spot is the ending, It is big, it is well-filmed, but it is also very abrupt. Perhaps there are no real loose ends to be tightened for the conclusion, but this sort of suddenness gives the impression that they simply ran out of film!

Film Daily called *The Misses Stooge* "a good number for putting lightness and laughter into a bill."[19] After the girls completed this movie, the Roach Studio had its annual shutdown. Patsy had become quite popular due to these short comedies, and secured work in three feature films, *Go Into Your Dance* with Al Jolson and Ruby Keeler, *Every Night at Eight* with George Raft and Alice Faye and *Page Miss Glory* with Marion Davies and Pat O'Brien. Thelma appeared in two B movies, *After the Dance* with Nancy Carroll and *Two for Tonight* with Bing Crosby and Joan Bennett. While Patsy received good notices for her work in the features, Thelma unfortunately appeared in two critical failures. They were the only films outside of the Roach comedies that Thelma appeared in that year.

The Misses Stooge was the last film James Parrott directed for Roach. His excesses had made him too unreliable. Stan Laurel hired him as a gag man and he contributed ideas to the Laurel and Hardy features *Way Out West, Swiss Miss* and *Block-Heads*, but he was otherwise unemployable. He died in 1939.

Slightly Static (1935)

Directed by William Terhune; *Produced by* Hal Roach; *Cinematographer:* Hap Depew; *Editor:* Ray Snyder; *Cast:* Thelma Todd, Patsy Kelly, Harold Waldridge, Dell Henderson, Nora Cecil, Carol Hughes, Ben Taggart, Louis

Natheaux, Elinor Vanderveer, Bobby Burns, Carl M. Leviness, Harry Bowen, Sydney Jarvis, Brooks Benedict, Aileen Carlyle, Dorothy Francis, Carlton Griffin, Kay Hughes, Sidney DeGray, Lorena Carr, Eddie Craven, The Sons of the Pioneers (Bob Nolan, Leonard Slye [Roy Rogers], Tim Spencer, Hugh Farr, Karl Farr), The Randall Sisters (Bonnie, Ruth and Shirley); *Released by* MGM on September 7, 1935; Two Reels

By the time *Slightly Static* was released, the August arrest of extortionist Harry Schimanski had put Thelma Todd's mind at ease. She felt a new sense of freedom and began to engage in more social activities, from a barbecue at actor Pat O'Brien's house to the wedding of her actress friend Inez Courtney.

Slightly Static was directed by William Terhune, who had written *The Tin Man*. Terhune was mostly employed as an editor, but tried his hand at directing a few shorts during the 1935–36 season. His directorial career was short-lived, but he did direct the three Todd–Kelly comedies.

Trying to break into radio, Thelma and Patsy trek to New York, get into a studio and try to attract attention. Thelma is interested in presenting dramatic readings, while Patsy has a soft shoe tap routine. It is not explained how Patsy's dancing will be a success on radio. But every time anyone walks by, or some music is heard in the background, Patsy goes into her dance.

This premise allows Patsy to show her prowess as a dancer, which had been her first foray into show business. She stated in an interview, "I was always spinning and tripping about the house, usually over chairs."[20] Patsy was so adept at tap dancing, she was teaching others by the age of 13. Thelma is again presented as haughty and pretentious, exhibiting skills in an elite, aloof manner.

The Roach Studio liked to do musical revue shorts, and explored this premise frequently with Our Gang. The kids' comedies *Our Gang Follies of 1936* and *Reunion in Rhythm* are among those involving musical numbers, while *Mike Fright* and *Pinch Singer* dealt with radio. *Slightly Static* seems to be, at least partially, an excuse to showcase musical acts the Randall Sisters and the Sons of the Pioneers.

The Randall Sisters—Bonnie, Ruth, and Shirely—were born in Mississippi and their hillbilly-flavored music was embraced by New York radio listeners as something different. They debuted as guests on Rudy Vallee's popular radio show, and later began working regularly with Paul Whiteman's orchestra. The Sons of the Pioneers was one of the earliest western singing groups. There were many lineup changes since they first formed in 1933. Roy Rogers had been in the act, and is seen in this film. At other times, Ken Curtis,

Shug Fisher and Pat Brady were members. The Sons of the Pioneers were still active in the 21st century.

There is some amusing dialogue in *Slightly Static* along with the slapstick and various musical interludes:

THELMA: At last we're in radio
PATSY: Yeah, we're in, now all we need is a job.

And:

THELMA: In Joplin, we stopped the show
Patsy: No, that was the censors

But the most interesting aspect of *Slightly Static* is how we're allowed, comedically, to take a look at how radio shows were performed.

Thelma and ZaSu are finally added to a radio show, and we see how they must respond to sound effects and props and speak in different voices. Thelma accidentally drinks a glass of shampoo, left over from an ad, causing soap bubbles to come out of her mouth as she speaks. When they are told there is only a minute left of the broadcast, Patsy starts rattling off the dialogue quickly and everyone tries hard to hurry through the remainder of the story so they can finish within the time.

Slightly Static is both interesting and funny, with a radio premise making a good framework for Thelma and Patsy's style of comedy. The musical interludes might make it seem a bit uneven, but overall the short is sufficiently entertaining.

Todd's private life was once again disrupted when in the fall of 1935, a mentally challenged man named Edward Schiffert admitted to writing the extortion letters, proving his hand-writing was a perfect match. He

Patsy Kelly and Thelma Todd in *Slightly Static* (1935).

129

claimed to have been in love with Todd, although he'd never met her. Schiffert admitted to "worshipping" Thelma's publicity photos and magazine photo layouts. He was committed to an asylum, and the charges against Schimanski were dropped.

The negative publicity that Thelma's private affairs garnered in the tabloid press was counterbalanced by the many positive things in her life. The minister of her church spoke to the press about Thelma's giving nature, especially when it came to children of the parish. Word got out that she always remembered her family back in Lawrence with gifts and letters. She continued to be unfailingly supportive of Mae Whitehead, a loyal employee. Mae's son fondly recalled for Michelle Morgan, 80 years after the fact, an expensive overcoat Thelma bought for him when he was a little boy.

When Patsy first began getting offers to appear in films outside of the comedy series, she took on every role. However, she now believed she was spreading herself too thin, and was becoming exhausted. After filming her scenes for the Warner Brothers feature *Thanks a Million*, she took no more work outside of the short comedy series for the remainder of 1935.

Thelma, however, agreed to take a supporting role in the Laurel and Hardy feature *The Bohemian Girl*, which was to go into production soon. But she first needed to negotiate with Hal Roach, and with Stan Laurel, regarding her role in the movie, and what her billing would be.

Twin Triplets (1935)

Directed by William Terhune; *Produced by* Hal Roach; *Cinematographer:* Art Lloyd; *Editor:* William Ziegler; *Cast:* Thelma Todd, Patsy Kelly, Greta Meyer, John Dilson, Billy Bletcher, Bess Flowers, James C. Morton, Charlie Hall, Grace Goodall, Charley Rogers; *Released by* MGM on October 12, 1935; Two Reels

In one of their earlier short comedy films, *Alum and Eve*, Thelma and ZaSu tell a fib to get out of trouble with a cop, but it ends up with them in a hospital, throwing it into chaos. A similar premise was used for Thelma and Patsy Kelly in *Twin Triplets*. They take a simple set-up to get into a hospital and it results in a series of comic situations.

Reporter Thelma wants to land a big scoop and prove herself. She hears about a parachute jumper whose chute did not open, but he survived the fall with injuries. She and Patsy cannot afford a streetcar to get to the hospital so that Thelma can secure an interview, so Thelma pretends to faint and Patsy screams for an ambulance. They figure this will get them a free ride to the hospital, and once they're in the building, they can sneak away and get the story.

The attempt to get an ambulance sets up a few gags. The first time this is attempted, it happens to be in front of a pet store. The owner runs inside to fetch a full fish bowl and dumps the water on Thelma to revive her. The second time works, and they get to the hospital. However, when Thelma finally finds the injured parachute jumper, he is so bandaged up that his muffled voice is incomprehensible. He is also quite mad, laughing uproariously as he tells his story. Thelma is unable to understand a word.

Meanwhile, a gruff-looking lady doctor, washing her hands while a lit cigarette dangles from her mouth (offering a great visual image), mentions having delivered six babies in the past hour. Patsy overhears the gist of this and concludes that a woman in the hospital gave birth to septuplets. She alerts Thelma, Thelma calls the paper, the editor arrives with a photographer, and things are all set for a big story for which Thelma has negotiated a great salary. When Patsy discovers her error, a fuming Thelma tells her to gather six random babies so they can somehow pull off the story. Thelma tells Patsy to find six babies and make it snappy and Patsy replies, "Where am I supposed to find six snappy babies?"

There is an amusing bit between Thelma and a German mother-to-be: Thelma asks if the woman has given birth to sextuplets and the woman answers, "Nein!" Patsy responds, "Not nine, six!" And when Patsy dons a nurse outfit and gathers six

Poster for *Twin Triplets* (1935).

babies from the maternity ward, she lines them up, gets into a bed pretending to be the mother, and the news people gather to take photos. Upon revealing each baby, they discover that one of them is black. The editor fires Thelma on the spot.

As with the aforementioned *Alum and Eve*, *Twin Triplets* starts with a simple basis and escalates into chaotic situations. It gets especially frantic while Patsy is trying to set up the six babies necessary to back up Thelma's claim. She thinks she has it, summons Thelma, she starts to gather the editor and photographer, but then Patsy waves her away, and Thelma must do likewise with the others. Patsy incorrectly concluded that the German woman was the mother of the alleged sextuplets. Realizing she won't be able to get this woman to play along with the ruse, Patsy then decides to pose as the mother. When the news people enter, Thelma's wild double-take reaction to Patsy being in the bed is one of the film's funniest moments. Patsy actually comes off as a bit more obnoxious in this film than in previous ones; there are scenes toward the end where she is screaming at the top of her lungs, but it is still funny.

There is one rather unsettling line of dialogue. The angry editor tells Thelma, "If you come into my office again, there will be a story, but you won't cover it. It'll be your murder!" In the wake of what happened to Thelma only months after this film's release, this dialogue can make a viewer uncomfortable.

Grace Goodall offers a strikingly outrageous visual as the smoking maternity doctor, James C. Morton as the heavily bandaged parachutist is delightfully nutty, and John Dilson, fairly new to films at this time, is very good as the harried editor. German-born Greta Meyer has a fun scene with Patsy that takes advantage of her first language. Wild and funny, *Twin Triplets* went over exceptionally well with audiences. Exhibitors called it one of Thelma and Patsy's best and stated that the audience laughed loudly throughout.

Patsy followed up this comedy with an appearance in the 20th Century–Fox feature *Thanks a Million* featuring Dick Powell and Ann Dvorak. Thelma was preoccupied with her personal life. Now that she no longer had to withdraw from social activities (her threatening extortionist was behind bars), she was rekindling her romantic connection to Roland West, even sparking rumors in the press that they were to be wed. West was still married to silent movie actress Jewel Carmen, so this rumor was troublesome for both West and Thelma.

The Todd–West collaboration continued to concentrate on the success of the Sidewalk Café, including adding an upstairs area for fine dining, which was much different than the more casual, relaxed atmosphere of the diner itself. There was also a lounge where celebrities stopped in for cocktails, secluded from the general population in the diner. But the Sidewalk Café also attracted mobsters who wanted to hold private gambling sessions afterhours. It is understood that such parties did occur among invited friends, but gangsters wanted a foothold onto this illegal activity and a piece of the action. Thelma was against this intrusion, and some speculate that this later resulted in trouble.

An ad slick used to promote a new Todd-Kelly comedy.

Thelma's career was also on her mind. Having made something of a name for herself, she believed it was time to branch out like her friend and former partner ZaSu Pitts and leave comedy shorts for more versatile roles. She fired her business manager, believing that she had the negotiating power to take care of her own contracts. Stan Laurel had returned to Roach after being allowed to produce his own films for his own unit. He began doing so with *Our Relations* (1936). First, Laurel wanted Thelma to appear in a feature film he was planning with Hardy, a comic version of Balfe's *The Bohemian Girl*. Thelma liked Laurel and Hardy and enjoyed working with them. She insisted, as part of her contract, that she would be billed second, right after the comedy team, in the credits. This was agreed upon.

Thelma planned to finish out her current contract of short subjects and then end her association with them. This time Roach did not balk as he had with ZaSu Pitts. Roach himself was planning to cease production on short films and concentrate solely on features. Laurel and Hardy made their last short, *Thicker Than Water*, in 1935. Charley Chase made his last short in 1936, then tried a feature entitled *Bank Night,* which ended up being edited down to two reels and released as a short. Chase then left the studio and set up shop at Columbia, where he starred in a new series of comedies, and directed shorts with the Three Stooges and Andy Clyde. Chase worked at Columbia until his death in 1940. The Our Gang series also ended at Roach in 1938; the producer then sold the series to MGM, including the name Our Gang (which is why the Roach films were called the Little Rascals on television).

Thelma realized short films were on their way out at Roach and she wanted to do more feature films. Patsy was doing quite well in her feature movie appearances. Even Thelma's fans were restless, writing to film magazines and inquiring why Thelma was still doing short comedies and not starring in major studio feature-length films. Roach wanted Thelma to appear in features for his company, which is one of the reasons why she was asked to appear in *The Bohemian Girl.*

Hot Money (1935)

Directed by James Horne; *Produced by* Hal Roach; *Cinematographer:* Art Lloyd; *Editor:* Louis McManus; *Cast:* Thelma Todd, Patsy Kelly, James Burke, Fred Kelsey, Louis Natheaux, Brooks Benedict, Hooper Atchley, Charlie Hall, Lee Phelps, Anya Tranda, Monte Vandergrift, Sherry Hall, Lee Prather, Tony Campanaro, Bobby Dunn; *Released by* MGM on November 16, 1935; Two Reels

With *Hot Money,* James Horne was back in the director's chair, his first since the Thelma Todd–ZaSu Pitts comedy *Red Noses.* And while *Red Noses* remains one of the best Todd Pitts efforts, *Hot Money* is decidedly one of the lesser shorts with Thelma and Patsy Kelly.

The film starts out typically enough. The landlord descends upon Thelma and Patsy and demands the back rent by nine p.m. or they will be evicted. When Patsy angrily shoves him, he changes the time to eight p.m., after which Patsy replies, "What a diplomat!" Patsy then starts to rub a lamp and wishes for $50,000. She is doing so in jest, but when a crook bursts into their apartment, throws $50,000 in cash, and says, "If I don't come back, you can keep it," Patsy thinks there might be something truly magical about the lamp. The man takes the keys and locks the girls in their apartment, but almost immediately runs into a rival gangster who shoots and kills him.

The remainder of the movie is pure farce. Patsy and Thelma believe they are indirectly responsible for the murder, because Patsy rubbed the lamp in hopes he never came back for the money. A couple of incompetent cops conduct an investigation, and do little more than stumble over obvious clues and get nowhere. The rival gangster is lurking about the apartment building in an effort to find where the dead man stashed the money. It amounts to a lot of entrances, exits, mistaken identities and slapstick gags. There are some isolated funny ideas strewn throughout, but the film concludes with several loose ends still hanging. This burlesque of the popular murder mysteries ultimately falls flat. Perhaps the concept offered too much plot for two reels.

The highlights are few. When the crook drops off the money, he says to Patsy, "You'll need it for a facelift." When Patsy realizes the man has been murdered, she claims, "I wasn't wishing for him to be dead, I was wishing he'd forget the address!" The crooks are dark and wily, the cops are bumbling and inept. James Burke and Fred Kelsey both played cops in many films, and often, even in comedies, they are gruff and controlling. Here, Burke is pushy but incompetent, and Kelsey is a yes-man who is even more inept. They are amusing and play off of Patsy's irascibility well.

The conflict between Thelma and Patsy has to do with the money itself. Patsy is all for keeping the money, especially since the only one who realizes they have it is dead. Thelma attempts to be the voice of reason, believing that since the money is obviously stolen, they should not keep stolen goods. Patsy's reaction is understandable in context, while Thelma's is noble. However, their attempt to return the money to law enforcement becomes complicated. The haphazard proceedings makes it difficult to do the right thing without being implicated in robbery and murder, despite their innocence.

While often Patsy's comedy could be a bit noisy and frantic, it seems to be amusingly so in *Hot Money*. Thelma is once again the stabilizing figure and offsets Patsy's exuberance effectively, but their cohesion doesn't extend to the film's overall structure. It offers a lot of set-ups, but not enough conclusions. The ending is abrupt (the rival gangster is arrested and taken away), and that is the only narrative element that is wrapped up. It is the central one, but not the only one.

Kelly told the author in 1976, "Thelma always kept me under control. If I got a little too loud, she told me to tone it down. If I wasn't loud enough, she told me to turn it up. We had so much fun making these pictures, I almost felt guilty taking the money."

Thelma and Patsy were actresses who did comedy and followed a director's orders. They would come up with ideas, of course, but did not have the filmmaking vision of some of their contemporaries. In fact, one of the reasons

Gus Meins was taken from their series and given to Our Gang was because it was felt that having a consistent directorial style would be easier for the kids' response to their own material.

The premise of *Hot Money*, with a lot of farcical activity within the framework of a comical murder mystery, is quite promising. But its concept is more interesting than its content. It is quick, brash and sometimes exciting, but overall it is not as good as some of the other Todd–Kelly comedies.

Hot Money was to be the last of Thelma Todd's movies to be released during her lifetime. She was found dead exactly one month after this film's release. Her death made headlines, especially due to the suspicious nature of it, and moviegoers were saddened by her passing. Despite the next couple of shorts being released posthumously, the Thelma Todd–Patsy Kelly comedies remained popular with moviegoers. In fact their next film, *Top Flat*, turned out to be one of their best.

Top Flat (1935)

Directed by William Terhune, Jack Jevne; *Produced by* Hal Roach; *Cinematographer:* Art Lloyd; *Editor:* Louis McManus; *Cast:* Thelma Todd, Patsy Kelly, Grace Goodall, Fuzzy Knight, Ferdinand Munier, Harry Bernard, Garry Owen, Henry Hall, Buddy Roosevelt, Bobby Burns, David Sharpe; *Released by* MGM on December 21, 1935; Two Reels

William Terhune returned to the director's chair for *Top Flat,* and was accompanied by Jack Jevne, a writer. Something worked, because *Top Flat* is one of the funnier Todd–Kelly two-reel comedies.

Once again we have a film that examines the duo's relationship. Thelma sits at a table pretentiously writing poetry, believing she has the talent and vision to get somewhere with her creativity. Patsy, ironing and making wisecracks, is fed up with Thelma's failure to contribute to the household. Annoyed, Thelma decides to pack her things and move. Thelma has delusions that her poems can net her some recognition while Patsy, remaining in the immediate working world, dismisses the concept as silliness. She mocks Thelma and her poetry. Thelma, sitting in creative mode, comes up with the line "Upon the door, a knock," and Patsy retorts, "It's the landlord looking for the rent while you write that poetry!" This mocking continues as Thelma packs to leave, with Patsy saying, "I suppose you'll be riding in a limo covered in furs!" This is a good example of comic foreshadowing.

The next scene shows Thelma working in a rich penthouse as a French maid for a wealthy couple, the Lamonts. During the 1930s, it was something of a status symbol to have a French maid—somehow this alluded to a higher social standing, a more cosmopolitan appearance. Thelma, of course, is merely playing French, obviously doing so to keep the job. Her entire Gallic expression is responding with "oui oui, madame," or monsieur, as the case may be. Once this is established, Thelma is told to

Thelma Todd in *Top Flat* (1935).

bring a mink coat downtown for a fitting. She travels by chauffeur and wears the mink. Patsy, a delivery girl en route to drop off a package, sees Thelma emerge from the limo wearing the fur and concludes that the poetry actually did pay off.

Kudos must be offered to the director(s) for the establishing shot of the penthouse in which Thelma works. The scene cuts from Thelma packing and leaving, to the penthouse, with an establishing shot that shows not only its vastness but also the wealth that exudes from the set design. The camera remains in a long to medium shot as Thelma enters the frame in a maid's outfit.

Once Patsy and Thelma are reunited, Patsy is so excited by Thelma's obvious success, she gushes passionately. Thelma can't bring herself to tell the truth, so she lets Patsy believe as she pleases. Once Thelma walks into the furrier, Patsy asks the chauffeur for her address, and later that night shows up with some rowdy friends. The penthouse owners are conveniently away, and Thelma is dressed in regular clothes, so the ruse continues. Another nod must go to the direction as Patsy enters the penthouse and is shown, in a nice, flowing tracking shot, walking around exploring the opulence and wealth of her surroundings.

From this point, *Top Flat* becomes a series of noisy situations, with Patsy's rowdy friends making the most of their situation. They bang away at the piano, loudly singing, Patsy joins them as Thelma fumes. The front desk calls due to others complaining about the noise. Thelma answers with "oui

oui," and when Patsy wonders why, Thelma replies, "because it's a French phone."

The two men drop water-filled bags off the balcony onto pedestrians below, while Patsy chooses to take a bath, phoning friends from the tub and saying, "Guess where I am!" Thelma can take no more. She admits to Patsy that she is only the maid, and her employers will be home any minute. Patsy tries to help Thelma, but the Lamonts arrive home.

Top Flat goes from slapstick to farce as Thelma goes to get Patsy's clothes from the bedroom and runs into Mr. Lamont. She tosses the clothes behind her, but they glide along the bathroom floor and end up down the chute. Patsy must leave the tub with a towel and hide in a closet, where she dons a pair of the heavyset Mr. Lamont's pajamas. Meanwhile, the rowdy friends drop a bag of water on a cop, who looks up and spots them. The farcical element continues as Thelma hurries from room to room trying to avoid the proprietor, while Patsy nearly gets caught and hides in one of the beds. Lamont believes that Patsy, hiding under the covers, is his wife and asks her to help him remove his shoes. When he gets no response, he dismisses it as his wife's moodiness. When he walks into another room and sees Mrs. Lamont, he returns to the bedroom to find Thelma standing near the bed. Hilariously, he concludes that Thelma had been hiding in the bed waiting for him. Mr. Lamont is played by older, fat, bald Ferdinand Munter, so the very idea that an attractive woman like Thelma would have designs on him is outrageously funny. Perhaps had Thelma been a gold digger. It is obvious that such a thing doesn't matter at all to Lamont. He is ready to make some plans, and starts doing so as his wife walks in. She responds with fury, chasing him around the penthouse. This allows Thelma and Patsy to escape. The cop sees this tumult and concludes that the Lamonts came home drunk and it is they who were dropping bags of water off their balcony.

Top Hat is one of the funnier Todd–Kelly comedies, with good situations and a lot of isolated gags that enhance its structure. The set-ups work beautifully. First, Thelma, who has not brought home any money in six weeks, is in conflict with hard-working Patsy who just got a raise. This leads to the mistaken idea that Thelma ended up wealthy. Patsy has no hard feelings, but the set-up of Thelma alone in a fancy penthouse that is not hers is met nicely with the arrival of Patsy and the two men. These men are tangential to the central theme of the film, but their boorishness accents the comedy nicely. They have no manners, no couth. They simply storm in, sit at the piano, and start loudly banging away, with no concern over the noise.

Slapstick is presented via the dropping of water bags. Their victims' reactions are individual. A kissing couple is unfazed. A haughty society man complains that such activity is "not cricket." Another man does a flip upon being hit. At the same time, Patsy is amusing in the bath (when she first sees the enormous tub, she asks, "Where's the diving board?"). She sits comfortably, with a bathing cap on and her foot up on the edge of the tub, delightedly phoning friends and, quite literally, soaking in the surrounding luxury. Some of the most outrageous slapstick occurs when Lamont walks into the bathroom while Patsy is still in the

Patsy Kelly in *Top Flat* (1935).

tub. Thelma pushes Patsy underwater and claims she is cleaning the tub. She must keep Patsy underwater until Lamont leaves. Patsy is nearly drowned after being submerged for almost 20 seconds.

When the film moves to farce and concentrates on the opening and closing of doors, the entering of and exiting from rooms, the pace picks up even further. The roly-poly Mr. Lamont, who waddles about with a big belly, is quite delusional to think young, pretty Thelma would be making advances to him, but it does show the wealthy perspective that anything is accessible to a rich man.

Top Flat is often a study in contrasts. There is the usual contrast between hard-working Patsy and dreamer Thelma. There is the contrast between the well-behaved Thelma and Patsy with her noisy, boorish friends. And central to the entire film is the contrast between wealth and working class. Haughty pretention is one extreme, while classless noisiness is the other. Thelma is caught in-between.

Ferdinand Munier only acted in a few Roach productions among the 100-plus films in which he appeared during his long career. Grace Goodall, who also played in just a handful of Roach films, appears as Mrs. Lamont. The boorish men are Garry Owen and Fuzzy Knight. Owen appeared in no other Roach films (he does appear with Laurel and Hardy in their later MGM film *Nothing But Trouble*), and is best remembered as the cab driver with the funny closing line in *Arsenic and Old Lace*. Knight was a noted Western film sidekick for much of his career (not to be confused with Al "Fuzzy" St. John). Among the water-bag victims, we see Roach stalwarts Bobby Burns, Harry Bernard and David Sharpe.

Top Flat was the first film released after Thelma Todd's death. Exhibitors indicated that the film went over well with moviegoers, and they would often ask if this was the last film Todd appeared in. It was not. *Top Flat* was shot in the late summer-early fall of 1935, after which Thelma filmed her scenes for the Laurel and Hardy feature *The Bohemian Girl*. Once she completed her work on that project, she returned to co-star with Patsy Kelly in their next two-reeler *All American Toothache*, her final film.

All American Toothache (1936)

Directed by Gus Meins; *Produced by* Hal Roach; *Cinematographer:* Art Lloyd; *Editor:* Jack Ogilvie; *Cast:* Thelma Todd, Patsy Kelly, Mickey Daniels, Johnny Arthur, Duke York, Billy Bletcher, Bud Jamison, Si Jenks, David Sharpe, Ray Cooke, Ben Hall, Sue Gomes, Charlie Hall, Buddy Messinger, Manny Vezie, Jack Cooper; *Released by* MGM on January 25, 1936; Two Reels

All American Toothache began production shortly after work completed on *The Bohemian Girl*. Thelma was perhaps at the height of her career. She was about to wrap up her short films series and it was already determined that Roach would have room for her in feature films. She also could pursue opportunities outside of the studio. And, off-screen, her restaurant continued to flourish. According to Michelle Morgan's book *The Ice Cream Blonde*, her café business "became such a mecca for celebrities that Thelma began acquiring special plates for them, personalized with their initials. Laurel and Hardy would drop in when they were at the beach, and friend Pat O'Brien was a regular visitor. Thelma loved the café so much that she ordered a variety of exclusive stationery items that sported her face and name, and plans were underway to add several more features to the establishment in the years ahead."[21]

Thelma's career and life was at its best. And while later stories indicate that gangsters intruded into her private life, the outside world, including her friends, all believed that things were going well.

Patsy Kelly was also eager to work in feature films, and some opportunities were already being considered. There were discussions that she and Thelma might appear in features as a team as well as separately.

All American Toothache is a comedy about dentistry, a premise that had become rather typical in slapstick comedy: Charlie Chaplin used this idea in his 1914 Keystone *Laughing Gas* and Stan Laurel gave it some attention in his 1923 solo short *White Wings*. Laurel, with Hardy, investigated the premise again in the 1927 two-reeler *Leave 'Em Laughing* and reworked the same material in the duo's 1931 feature *Pardon Us*. A year later, W.C. Fields starred as *The Dentist* in a Mack Sennett two-reeler.

All American Toothache features Mickey Daniels as a college football hero who cannot play in the big game unless he finishes his field experience in dentistry school. His assignment is that he must pull a wisdom tooth. Workers at a nearby diner frequented by college people, Thelma and Patsy are friends with the students and the faculty. When Thelma hears Mickey must pull a wisdom tooth, she recruits Patsy, who is duped into going along with the idea. Once Patsy is in the dentist's chair, her x-ray reveals a tooth whose extraction will require experts. The football team needs Mickey to

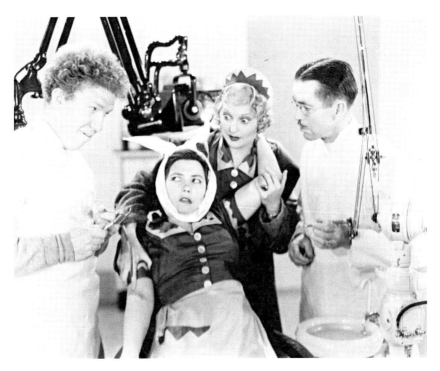

Left to right: Mickey Daniels, Patsy Kelly, Thelma Todd and Johnny Arthur in *All American Toothache* **(1936).**

make the extraction, so they confront the dentist. A free-for-all erupts and Mickey does pull a wisdom tooth, but it is from his dental instructor. However, technically, this is what he needed to do, so he is allowed to play in the big game—and he ends up losing it for his team by running the wrong way for a touchdown!

All American Toothache is a very funny comedy and a rather unusual one in the Todd–Kelly filmography. Thelma and Patsy are supporting characters to the central premise: Mickey Daniels and his need to pull a wisdom tooth. If the film more accurately followed the established formula, Patsy would be the one needing to pull the tooth and Mickey would be the unwilling patient.

The film opens with the set-up of Mickey needing to complete his dental experience with the pulling of a wisdom tooth. Thelma and Patsy are not on screen until the next scene when Mickey and his coach are in the diner, complaining about their situation, and leading Thelma to recruit Patsy as the hapless patient. There are a few amusing visual ideas as the premise is being built upon. To convince Patsy to allow Mickey to pull her tooth, Thelma brings up a silver tray that allows a mirror-like reflection, but distorts the image to appear that one cheek is sticking out. When Patsy sees this distorted reflection, she is convinced that an abscess has formed and that she must arrange to have that tooth pulled.

Another neat visual is when Patsy's tooth is x-rayed. An animated image of a very impacted tooth is shown, causing the dental instructor to insist on specialists performing the extraction. He claims that if Mickey tries to engage in a complicated extraction like this, "he might take your jawbone too!"

All American Toothache features some of the usual gags that seem to appear in every comedy about a dentist. While Patsy is in the waiting room before going through with the procedure, she overhears two plumbers working on some pipes in an adjacent room. Believing they are the dentists, Patsy reacts big when she hears that "the drill got stuck" during the procedure. She is relieved upon entering the other room and realizing she was listening to plumbers.

The free-for-all is nicely filmed with returning director Gus Meins editing quickly between shots at different lengths and angles. It is brief, but funny, and the idea to conclude the film with Mickey's mishap is a neat touch. The final shot is a close-up tracking shot of Mickey happily running with the football, with the headline that indicates he ran the wrong way.

Daniels was something of a Hal Roach Studios veteran, having worked in silent Our Gang comedies and the Boy Friends series. He last appeared with Thelma and ZaSu Pitts in their first short comedy, *Let's Do Things*. While he was no longer in a regular series at Roach, he frequently came back to do cameos. Duke York, who plays the coach, is probably better known for appearing in several Three Stooges comedies, often playing a hulking brute at odds with the boys, most notably in *Who Done It* (1949). Johnny Arthur, who plays the dental instructor, appeared in a handful of *Our Gang* comedies, sometimes as Darla Hood's harried father.

The return of Gus Meins behind the camera helped make *All American Toothache* one of the funniest in the Todd–Kelly series. Meins, who had recently won the Diploma d'Honneur from the International Festival de Cinema at Brussels, Belgium, wanted to expand his scope at Roach and no longer be limited to one series. As Roach planned to move into feature film production, Meins wanted to investigate possibilities in this area, allowing him to advance his own skills and opportunities.

That *All American Toothache* is one of the funnier Todd–Kelly comedies, makes it all the more unfortunate that it turned out to be Thelma's final movie. The prospect of this team entering feature film production after they finished off the few two-reelers left on their contract is something we can only speculate.

The Death
of Thelma Todd

This is not a book that will attempt to understand or use evidence to conclude anything about Thelma Todd's tragic, untimely death. There are biographies that provide such information, and speculation, and one can refer to this book's bibliography for any of those books. However, even in a study of her films, Todd's death has to be discussed. It was a heartbreaking end to a comedy series that had real momentum and impact.

Based on the information available from various sources, on a Saturday night not long after filming completed on *All American Toothache*, Todd went to a party while Roland West tended to the restaurant. He told her to return home by two a.m. She defiantly said she'd return home at 2:05. West later recalled that this conversation was done in a joking manner, and he was not giving her orders or an ultimatum. There was nothing threatening about his demand.

Thelma was dropped off by her chauffeur, Ernest Peters, at a party at the Trocadero club on Saturday, December 14, at 8:25 p.m. Her ex-husband Pat De Cicco was at the party with his new girlfriend, actress Margaret Lindsey. Depending on which account you read, Thelma was either angry about this or unconcerned. She had dinner, spent time talking to friends like actress Ida Lupino and, according to accounts, was in good spirits and not intoxicated. At around 1:55 a.m., she asked her friend, restaurateur Sid Grauman, to phone West at the café and indicate she was soon to be leaving for home. However, she got involved in a conversation with British actor Stanley Lupino (Ida's father) and didn't leave for home until after three a.m. Her friend, actor and dancer William Prince, walked Thelma to her car where chauffeur Peters was waiting.

Peters drove Thelma home and they arrived at her place at around 3:45 a.m. She left the car, and Peters was about to escort her to her apartment, but she said that wasn't necessary. On Monday morning, December 16, 1935,

Todd's body was found in her car, parked in the garage, by her maid, Mae Whitehead. Thelma was only 29 years old. When the police arrived, they noticed rigor mortis had started to set in, indicating that the body had been there for some time. She died of carbon monoxide poisoning from sitting in a car that was running with no ventilation. An investigation began immediately, but the case was never solved. Now, in the 21st century, it is still an intriguing unsolved mystery. There are many theories as to how Thelma Todd died, and these can be found in any number of the aforementioned biographies. Some claim she was murdered. Others believe she committed suicide. Still others think it was a tragic accident.

Thelma had been to lunch with erstwhile screen partner and longtime friend ZaSu Pitts only days earlier. ZaSu was shocked and saddened to hear of Thelma's death. Patsy Kelly had a complete emotional breakdown and had to be hospitalized. Thelma had purchased and mailed out Christmas cards days before she died. Charley Chase received his shortly after hearing of her death, and reportedly broke down in uncontrollable sobs. Funeral services were held at the Wee Kirk o' Heather in Glendale with Dr. Harold Proppe speaking informally on the life of the actress. Cremation followed.

Only days later, Hal Roach announced to the trades that he planned to continue the comedy series with Patsy Kelly. However, it was also decided to re-edit the Laurel and Hardy feature *The Bohemian Girl* and cut out Thelma's scenes. The role of the Gypsy princess was instead played by elderly Zeffie Tilbury in new footage that was shot and added to the film. The romance with actor Antonio Moreno was changed over to Mae Busch, who also played Hardy's wife. Despite the removal of Thelma's scenes, and the addition of newly shot footage, *The Bohemian Girl* came off okay. None of Laurel and Hardy's scenes appear to have been altered. It is not known why it was decided to remove Thelma, but perhaps Roach felt her recent tragic death would impact upon the success of the film. He did not however, withhold her last two short comedies with Patsy Kelly from posthumous release. Kelly recalled for the author in 1976: "When Thelma died, it broke my heart. It broke all of our hearts. We tried to continue making the pictures but it just wasn't the same."

Actress Pert Kelton was hired to take Thelma's place in the next short, *Pan Handlers*. Trade announcements at the time were conflicting. Some articles indicate that Pert was hired to complete the series of three more shorts on Patsy's contract, while others claim that she was only hired for one film. According to a February 18, 1936, *Variety* article, "Roach is building up a new comedy team of Pert Kelton and Patsy Kelly to replace the late Thelma Todd–Patsy Kelly combo. Kelton will appear in the last of a series of two-reelers staring this week." However, two days earlier, *Motion Picture Daily* stated that Kelton would take Thelma's place in the next short, which would go into production on February 20: "Miss Kelton has not been signed to complete the series, but has been engaged just for this short." Kelton did appear opposite Kelly in *Pan Handlers*, her only film in the series. After that, Patsy was teamed with Lyda Roberti for two more shorts and the contracted number of two-reel comedies was completed.

6

The Film of Patsy Kelly and Pert Kelton

Pan Handlers (1936)

Directed by William Terhune; *Produced by* Hal Roach; *Cinematographer:* Art Lloyd; *Editor:* William Ziegler; *Cast:* Patsy Kelly, Pert Kelton, Rosina Lawrence, Grace Goodall, Estelle Etterre, Dave Sharpe, Harry Bowen, Chester Gan, Rube Clifford, Larry Steers; *Released by* MGM on February 29, 1936; *Working title: Pot Luck;* Two Reels

Pert Kelton was a vaudeville performer with a knack for comedy. She had been in movies since the dawn of the sound era, repeating her Broadway role as Rosie in the 1929 film version of the musical *Sally*. Throughout the early 1930s, she appeared in several RKO films, including *Lightning Strikes Twice* with Thelma Todd and *Sing and Like It* with ZaSu Pitts. Pert had a wise-cracking style similar to Patsy Kelly's and it was decided that she could perhaps work well with her. Unfortunately, there is little chemistry to be found with this teaming. Patsy carries the film and Pert offers meager support. They even dyed her hair blonde to look more like Thelma and to offer the contrast opposite Patsy. Thelma's characters' more calm and rational demeanor had played off of Patsy's brashness much better. Pert's demeanor seems more similar to a toned-down version of Patsy.

The story follows the basic formula that had already been established. Pert and Patsy, low on money, attend a sales meeting where they are convinced by the presenter that they can make big money selling the pots and pans that she represents. This trained representative tells the crowd gathered for her presentation that if they buy a complete set, they'll have no problem selling it for a profit. Ensuing sales will net them even more money. Pert and Patsy take the bait.

The premise is interesting in that such companies still exist in the 21st century. One noted product will hold similar meetings and entice you to go around demonstrating a product at people's homes, with the understanding that you will be paid after 50 demonstrations. If you only manage to do 49, you get nothing. It is a sham, of course, and during the Depression desperate people would fall for such a ruse. Pert and Patsy are playing people like those.

Pert and Patsy go door to door, offering a few amusing situations. When a Chinese man comes to the door, they try to slowly and loudly explain their reason for knocking, believing he might have trouble understanding English. The Chinese man responds to them with perfect English eloquence. At another stop, they try in vain to communicate with a man who is very hard of hearing, and believes they want to rent his house. After several minutes of amusing misunderstandings, they discover he has a similar set of pots and pans that he was never able to unload. They also end up at the home of the woman who gave the presentation. They ask for their money back, and she refuses.

These scenes allow Pert and Patsy to play off a disparate group of char-

Left to right: Pert Kelton and Patsy Kelly in *Pan Handlers* (1936). Pert replaced the deceased Thelma Todd, but for only this film.

acters. Pert is unable to say the word "aluminum" so, when Pert makes her pitch, every time she comes to that word, Patsy says it for her.

Pan Handlers shifts gears when Pert and Patsy come to the home of a harried young housewife who has to cook dinner for her husband and some guests, but has no idea how. Pert and Patsy agree to cook the dinner as a demonstration of their wares, with the understanding that the housewife will then purchase a set from them.

Pert and Patsy have a great deal of trouble in the kitchen. First, the turkey they are roasting shrinks. They decide to remedy it with stuffing, and some yeast chips fall into the bird. As they are preparing to stuff it, they see out the window that their sales rep nemesis lives next door and is cooking a large turkey. They sneak into her house and steal the turkey, leaving their shrunken one behind. This results in a lot of back-and-forth. A dog gets away with the large turkey, while the shrunken one expands from the yeast. However, when the dinner is served, one stab of a fork into the turkey causes it to explode.

The second reel of this two-reel comedy owes more to farce than slapstick. The stealing and re-stealing of the turkey, the woman coming over and chasing the girls around the table while the homeowners and guests watch in confusion, and the explosive ending, are all outrageously amusing. But this amusement is very superficial. Kelton, a fine comic in her own right, just does not gel with Patsy, who is trying her best to carry the proceedings.

Audiences liked this teaming and this short. Exhibitors reported that their patrons laughed loudly throughout the movie, and even stated that they looked forward to the next Kelton–Kelly comedy. But there would be no more.

There are two standouts in the supporting cast. Grace Goodall, adept at playing haughty, reserved characters, scores as the sales rep. The harried housewife is Rosina Lawrence, memorable for her roles in the Charley Chase short *On the Wrong Trek* (1936) and the Laurel and Hardy feature *Way Out West* (1937).

The month after this movie was released, the trades announced that Kelly would hereafter be making only feature-length movies. Roach was going to abandon the idea of having Patsy finish out the short subjects left on her contract. He realized that Thelma's death left too much of a void.

Apparently the producer changed his mind. A formidable candidate to team with Kelly came along in the form of Lyda Roberti. Another blonde, though with a character that was far different from Thelma Todd's, Roberti was a hit Broadway star and scored in the film *Million Dollar Legs* featuring

W.C. Fields, Jack Oakie and a host of familiar comedians like Hugh Herbert and Andy Clyde. The Polish-born actress usually played a hot-tempered seductress with a heavy accent. In her films with Patsy, she tries to fit in with the comedy team dynamic. She is no Thelma Todd, but is an improvement over Pert Kelton.

According to the trades, Lyda was supposed to appear in only one comedy, even though Patsy had two more to complete under her current contract. Another actress was to be hired for the next film. But Roberti worked well enough with Patsy, so she was hired to do the last film as well.

Kelton went on to do more films and eventually television. She was the first actress cast as Alice Kramden opposite Jackie Gleason in *The Honeymooners*, back when it was a short sketch on Gleason's variety show. By the time it became a series, Kelton was blacklisted, so Audrey Meadows was hired. Gleason always felt badly about that situation, and years later Kelton was hired to play Alice Kramden's mother in an episode. She remained active until her death in 1968. She died while swimming at the YWCA. Kelton was married and had two sons. Her husband lived another 30 years, dying in 1998.

Kelly's feelings about the series were less than enthusiastic. She told the author in 1976: "Once Thelma was gone, I just finished the pictures on our contract with some other girls and then Hal Roach put me in feature pictures. That was the plan, even when Thelma was alive. The girls who worked with me on those last pictures were great. No problems. But it just wasn't the same."

The Films of Patsy Kelly
and Lyda Roberti

At Sea Ashore (1936)

Directed by William Terhune; *Produced by* Hal Roach; *Cinematographer:* Art Lloyd; *Editor:* Ray Snyder; *Cast:* Patsy Kelly, Lyda Roberti, Al Shean, Robert Emmett O'Connor, Joe Twerp, Harry Bowen, Fred Kelsey, Leonard Kilbrick, Jack Hill, William J. O'Brien, The Avalon Boys (Don Brookins, Art Green, Walter Trask, Chill Wills); *Released by* MGM on April 4, 1936; *Working title: Mutiny on the Boundary;* Two Reels

Lyda Roberti's first film with Patsy Kelly was another experiment, as the teaming with Pert Kelton had been. Suppressing her unhappiness with the sad situation, Patsy told *Modern Screen* magazine:

> Lyda is very funny. You see, it's simple because Lyda, with her dialect, is so entirely different. She doesn't understand all the English words and that makes for comedy and it's easy to get laughs. The only change is that where Thelma used to play straight and I did the foil, the positions are reversed. I play straight and Lyda does the foil.[1]

Just as Patsy was welcomed and was treated with respect when she replaced ZaSu Pitts, she welcomed Lyda and put her at ease. She would rehearse with her for hours off-set to make sure everything would run smoothly.

Roberti came from a difficult background, living in Russia during the Revolution. Her father was a clown who traveled the world with circuses. Lyda related to Jack Smalley in *Movie Classic* magazine:

> I have never talked about my life, because so much of it is filled with bitterness. It makes my throat ache and then I cry when I should be clowning. Always, it seems, there were people trying to kill each other everywhere I would go. I have heard bullets go by my head, and seen people die. A circus burned and I escaped. A bridge blew up, yet I was lucky. We went on. And then the Americans came to stop the fighting. American soldiers ate at the camp. My father offered to put on shows if they would feed us. We spent a year in Japan and then three years in China. Many Americans there would say "You should come to America."[2]

Lyda finally made her way to the States and sang and danced her way to success: vaudeville, Broadway and eventually movies. Often playing vamps, Lyda longed to do music and comedy. She was, therefore, very pleased with the opportunity afforded her by an interested Hal Roach.

Roberti told the press that she was happy becoming part of a comedy team: "It is wonderful. Comedy is what I want to play on the screen. They always had me vamping and I don't like that. I will show them I am funny. Patsy is wonderful. She gives other people like me a break. Mr. Roach is wonderful. I can be funny instead of rolling my eyes at men."[3]

Patsy was merely finishing out her contract with the short comedies and eager to extend to feature films as well as pursue opportunities elsewhere. But she did her best and was respectful of Lyda.

Lyda Roberti (pictured) was first teamed with Patsy Kelly in *At Sea Ashore* (1936).

At Sea Ashore opens with Patsy working alone at a doughnut shop. When a mishap occurs that causes her boss Mr. Rumplemeyer to lose his only pair of pants, Patsy must take his place on an errand to pick up his visiting niece, Lyda, who is arriving by ship that day.

While Pert Kelton's initial appearance in *Pan Handlers* was alongside Patsy as an established connection, Lyda Roberti's first appearance in *At Sea Ashore* is alone, spotlighting her separately. She walks off the ship, stops where the Avalon Boys are doing an impromptu song, and joins them. She sings, she dances, and this is how the film establishes her. Pert was obviously part of a team, replacing Thelma, with her hair dyed blonde and her immediate connection to Patsy, their shared situation and eventual scheme. Lyda starts a new situation, a different dynamic. Patsy is alone, she meets her new cohort here. Lyda's number is, in fact, a distraction from the narrative and seems out of place.

The farcical construct remains with this film as Patsy arrives at the dock by cab (asking the driver to wait) and sneaks into the area in hopes of finding Lyda with the sketchiest description from Rumplemeyer. Throughout her search, she runs about and is continually confronted by different immigrants from various cultures, and she must somehow respond to each. There is verbal confusion due to the language barrier. At one point, an Apache dancer picks Patsy up and spins her around. Patsy eventually stumbles into Lyda, sitting patiently on a trunk.

The dynamic between Lyda and Patsy is immediately more cohesive than Pert Kelton and Patsy had been. Patsy's forceful personality works well with her now being in the leadership position of a duo situation, while Lyda's own charisma is limited by the cultural difference she displays as being new to the country.

The farcical element continues as a cop confronts the cab driver who is dutifully waiting for Patsy, the meter still running and the fare rising. The cop wants to give the cabbie a ticket for parking in a No Parking area, and is skeptical when the cab driver explains he is waiting for a fare. They go to where the ship is docked and the cabbie points out Patsy. Patsy, however, sees a cop and the cab driver and figures she must be in some kind of trouble, so she speaks broken English attempting to appear to be an immigrant. The cop is fooled, the cabbie gets a ticket, and Patsy gets away.

However, this leads to another situation. The immigration officer also believes Patsy is an immigrant and is not allowed to leave the area without a passport. This introduces a fun slapstick situation. Patsy hides in Lyda's trunk, and Lyda flirtatiously gets an officer to help her move the trunk out onto the sidewalk. He does so without regard to how violently he is bouncing it around, while Patsy gets banged about on the inside.

The film wraps up when Patsy is again confronted by immigration and by the cab driver to whom she owes money. Rumplemeyer arrives just in time and explains who Patsy is. This takes care of immigration, but when Rumplemeyer learns that she also owes a $20 cab fare that she can't pay, he insists he's never seen her before. This final scene is one of the funniest parts of the movie.

At Sea Ashore is essentially Patsy Kelly's movie, and she carries it successfully enough. There is not a lot of investigation as to how well she and Lyda Roberti can work as a team, but they have enough scenes together to offer at least some discernible chemistry. While it is nowhere near the cohesion Patsy had enjoyed with Thelma Todd, there is potential that Hal Roach obviously felt was worth further consideration. The short gets off to a very slow start, but once Patsy and Lyda meet, it gets going and ends up being fairly entertaining.

While this film was still in production, Roach viewed the dailies and felt that Lyda was working well with Patsy and that she should be retained for the final two-reeler to be produced with Patsy's current contract. Roach had big plans for Patsy. He was already planning to cast her in a feature that would also star Charley Chase, Rosina Lawrence and Guinn "Big Boy" Williams. Lyda, meanwhile, was considered for a contract. In the May 5, 1936, issue of *Film Daily*, it was announced, "Immediately after seeing the rushes on the first Patsy Kelly–Lyda Roberti comedy, Hal Roach yesterday signed Miss Roberti to a long-term contract. Miss Kelly and Miss Roberti will next be teamed in a feature-length production, *Girls Go West*."

Hill Tillies (1936)

Directed by Gus Meins; *Produced by* Hal Roach; *Cinematographer:* Art Lloyd; *Editor:* William Ziegler; *Cast:* Patsy Kelly, Lyda Roberti, Toby Wing, Harry Bowen, Sam Adams, James C. Morton, Dave Sharpe, Ronald Rondell, Jim Thorpe; *Released by* MGM on April 24, 1936; *Working title: Ha Ha Wilderness;* Two Reels

While Hal Roach was preparing to put together the feature *Girls Go West*, Patsy Kelly and Lyda Roberti finished out Patsy's contractual obligation of short subjects by starring in *Hill Tillies*. It presents the two of them in a full team dynamic, which allows us to see the genesis of this idea. Interestingly, while Patsy is the leader, she is also the nervous and manic member of the team while Lyda is calmer and more reserved. She also plays the airheaded foreigner stereotype, so she is oblivious to danger and her accent causes a communication conflict.

This dynamic is far different that what Thelma Todd and Kelly offered, and is also unlike the combination of Kelly and Pert Kelton. While it formed some basis in *At Sea Ashore*, apparently Hal Roach believed there was enough to explore further by putting the girls in feature films. This is due to the fact that Roach was switching exclusively to feature film production, save for the Our Gang comedies, which had been reduced to one-reelers. Gus Meins, who directed this short, was also moving to feature film production. He had helmed the Laurel and Hardy feature *Babes in Toyland* and was also set to direct *Girls Go West*.

Hill Tillies opens with the girls as part of a trio, as supporting player Toby Wing opens the film with them as a third roommate. Toby and Lyda are at their apartment when Patsy is carried in by the police, having fainted several blocks away. After the cops leave, Patsy reveals she was faking so she didn't have to walk all the way home. Once again low on money, Toby sees a newspaper article about a man who got a big payoff for spending a week in the wilderness. Toby decides that Patsy and Lyda will pull off such a stunt, while she and a sharpster promoter, her friend Joe, generate publicity. The premise is that women can survive in the wilderness just as effectively as men.

It is decided that once the reporters have taken pictures, Patsy and Lyda will enter the woods, and when the reporters leave, Toby and her operator friend will send in food and supplies to the girls so they can survive comfortably. While Toby Wing is part of the dynamic at the outset of the film, she is soon relegated to support. This allows Lyda and Patsy to establish their relationship.

Once the scene switches to the woodsy area that Patsy and Lyda are about to enter, they are surrounded by reporters while Joe stirs things up by talking about the dangers the girls will face. There is some fun dialogue:

REPORTER: Is it true you're not taking any rattlesnake cure?
LYDA: Why should we? If the snakes get sick, it's their problem
REPORTER: What'll you do if you see a black widow?
PATSY: Get her a husband.

Once the reporters leave, Patsy and Lyda go into the woods and sit on a log waiting for Toby and Joe to bring them supplies. Attempting to create fire by rubbing two rocks, and two sticks, together, an angry Patsy then tosses a rock toward some kindling. It skids along another rock and the sparks ignite the wood, creating a campfire.

As indicated above, Patsy is both the leader and the more nervous of the two. She is confronted by a lion after saying, "Nothing will make me move from this log," and runs away screaming. When they hear noises, Lyda decides they are Indians and tries to respond. A frightened Patsy stops her. When they see the tail feathers of turkeys sticking out in the brush, Lyda tries to call to the Indians and again a frightened Patsy quiets her. When Lyda sees the turkeys, she states, "Look, it's only an ostrich!"

Lyda Roberti and Patsy Kelly in a posed promotional shot. *Hill Tillies* **(1936) was their last short subject.**

Lyda's foreign accent and blissfully ignorant approach to the wild makes her carefree and unafraid. The more savvy Patsy is scared, perhaps mostly because this Brooklyn-born city girl is far out of her element. After being chased by the lion, Patsy is shown sleeping up in a tree, rolling over and falling out. Lyda, meanwhile, is happily swinging from a branch.

There is a funny bit when Toby and Joe send two Indian guides into the wilderness to find the girls and bring them their supplies. Patsy and Lyda see the men and Patsy fears they are about to be scalped. She has to explain to Lyda what scalping is.

LYDA: So what? The barber does that too.
PATSY: Yeah, but when the barber cuts your hair, he doesn't take off part of your head!

When the Indian guides find the girls, the older Indian is attracted to Patsy and dances around her. He feels her arms and happily says, "Big fat squaw!"

Patsy is insulted. The Indians have brought blankets, supplies and food. The next portion of the film shows the girls being confronted by a crazy hermit who insists he is looking for his horse. They play along with him in a rather lengthy scene reminiscent of the old Crazy House act often performed in burlesque.

Hill Tillies seems a bit trite, with rather predictable gag situations, but it was successful with audiences. *Film Daily* opined,

> The efforts of a couple of swell comics, Patsy Kelly and Lyda Roberti, make this two-reeler pleasing comedy entertainment. The girls work together well and given the proper material should make a grand team. The cast is especially good.... A scene with a crazy hermit is the highlight of the show, and when the ten days are over, the gals come out crazy too.[4]

The reviews made note of the fact that the older Indian, who had designs on Patsy, was played by former football star Jim Thorpe.

With this final short completed, Roach now wanted to produce feature films. Of his successful short comedy stars, only Laurel and Hardy had proven themselves in feature-length films. The Charley Chase feature *Bank Night* was edited down to two-reel length and released as *Neighborhood House*. Chase left Roach after 12 years of steady successful employment, but not before appearing in one more feature, *Kelly the Second*, in which his co-star was Patsy Kelly. Our Gang's feature attempt *General Spanky* was a flop. George "Spanky" McFarland told the author, "The success of Our Gang stemmed from the fact that we were regular kids in a neighborhood. *General Spanky* had us as kids in the Civil War. It was a stilted situation that just didn't fly."[5]

As a result, the Our Gang comedies returned to short subjects, now only one reel in length. An article in the June 13, 1936, *Hollywood Scene* indicated that Roach was to now exclusively produce feature films, along with the occasional Our Gang one-reeler. (Roach would soon sell that series to MGM.)

Patsy Kelly had a lot of work planned after completing *Hill Tillies*. She appeared in support of Robert Taylor and Loretta Young in the Fox feature *Private Number*. A couple of months later, she was given top billing in the Roach feature *Kelly the Second*, co-starring Charley Chase as well as several actors with whom Patsy had already worked, including Rosina Lawrence, Guinn "Big Boy" Williams and her one-time partner Pert Kelton. Patsy next appeared in Fox's *Sing Baby Sing* with Alice Faye, and then she had a very funny role in Fox's *Pigskin Parade* with Stuart Erwin, Jack Haley, Betty Grable and a young Judy Garland.

Kelly had now become very established as a strong supporting actor in major motion pictures. Her presence offered comic relief in more serious films and enhanced the comedies further. Her progress since first entering movies via the Roach-produced two-reelers opposite Thelma Todd was pretty impressive. At first tentative about slapstick and ready to leave movies altogether, Patsy had risen to the level of a sought-after character actress whose comic presence enhanced every film in which she appeared. Patsy also remained committed to her work at Roach and believed her future with Lyda Roberti was promising. So did Hal Roach.

Girls Go West was being prepared throughout the time that Patsy was busy with her other film commitments. Patsy and Lyda would be its stars and present their team dynamic in a full-length feature with supporting actors and production numbers. Roach borrowed notable supporting actors from other studios, including Robert Armstrong and Lynne Overman. Gus Meins was slated to direct. By the time it was ready to be released, the title was changed to *Nobody's Baby*.

Nobody's Baby (1937)

Directed by Gus Meins; *Produced by* Hal Roach; *Cinematographer:* Norman Brodine; *Editor:* Ray Snyder; *Cast:* Patsy Kelly, Lyda Roberti, Lynne Overman, Robert Armstrong, Rosina Lawrence, Don Alvarado, Tom Dugan, Orrin Burke, Dora Clement, Laura Treadwell, Wilma Cox, Ottola Nesmith, Joan Woodbury, Florence Roberts, Si Wills, Herbert Rawlinson, Walter Trask, Lois Wilde, Robert Winkler, Dennis O'Keefe, Cyril Ring, Larry Steers, Chick Chandler, Phyllis Crane, Lester Dorr, Bess Flowers, Daisy Bufford, Walter Clinton, Delos Jewkes, Pat Lane, Richard Kipling, Otto Maide, Carl M. Leviness, Charles Marsh, William H. O'Brien, Broderick O'Farrell, Field Norton, June Mishi, Dave Pepper, Stanley Price, Larry Wheat, William Henry Phen, Joseph Forte, Fay Holderness, Jack Hill, Eleanor Vanderveer, The Rhythm Rascals, The Avalon Boys, Jimmy Grier and his Orchestra; *Released by* MGM on April 23, 1937; *Working title: Girls Go West;* 68 minutes

Hal Roach believed the double feature was taking the place of running a feature attraction with short subjects. And while other studios continued making shorts into the 1950s, Roach concluded his short subject production in the 1930s. By switching to feature films exclusively, Roach was interested in using his established stars, so this full-length film was arranged for Patsy Kelly and Lyda Roberti.

Nobody's Baby benefits from being able to give Patsy and Lyda's characters more depth, to allow them a longer narrative to work in, and also open up the budget beyond the parameters of a two-reeler. Unfortunately, despite a good cast, director and screenwriters *Nobody's Baby* is only a fair comedy feature with a few amusing moments. What it does show is that Patsy and Lyda were perfectly capable of handling the starring roles in a feature production, so the future of their team seemed promising.

Patsy and Lyda do not play an established team at the outset of the film. Both are, in fact, going for the same job at a radio station. Lyda is interested in getting work as a singer. Patsy is a dancer, and does not appear to realize that dancing doesn't exactly work on radio. They end up doing a number together for an audition, because Lyda is summoned to perform and Patsy mistakenly believes it is she who was asked. So Lyda starts performing her song and the undaunted Patsy begins tap-dancing to the music. Neither gets the job. When Patsy gets a room at a boarding house, it turns out her roommate is Lyda. Despite initial differences, they end up friendly and go into the nursing profession together.

The dynamic between the two characters is nicely established and carries over from what they began to establish in their two-reelers. Patsy is loud, brassy and forceful. Lyda is good naturedly dense, easygoing and earnest. Their personalities blend cohesively. The plot is in regard to dancers Tony and Yvonne, who perform at a successful nightclub where Patsy and Lyda are attending with two reporters looking for a scoop about the dancing couple. Apparently, Tony and Yvonne are married and while Yvonne wants to make that known, Tony does

Poster for *Nobody's Baby* (1937).

159

not, and it is a sore subject between them. The reporters are interested in verifying that rumor and breaking the news. Yvonne walks out on Tony, putting the act in jeopardy. While she is away, Tony tries to work with a dancer who is all wrong for him, but stubbornly refuses to make up with Yvonne. Yvonne, however, gives birth in the hospital where Patsy and Lyda work. They agree to help her reconnect with Tony by letting him know he has a baby. Despite a series of complications, it all works out in the end.

While *Nobody's Baby* doesn't rise beyond the level of merely average, there are lot of factors here that work. First, the ability of Patsy and Lyda to carry the film as a team is most significant. While their characters are not central to the narrative, they are an important element and are instrumental in carrying it. And it was intelligent of Roach to secure the services of character actors Robert Armstrong and Lynne Overman for the reporter roles. Armstrong had well established himself in films like *King Kong* (1933) and the James Cagney vehicle *"G" Men* (1935) as a formidable character actor who could effectively punch up any scene. Overman had proven his adeptness at playing comedy with appearances in *Little Miss Marker* (1934), *Broadway Bill* (1934) and *Poppy* (1936). They work well with Patsy and Lyda without overshadowing them. As Tony and Yvonne, Hal Roach protégé Rosina Lawrence registers nicely opposite veteran actor Don Alvarado.

The film works best when it relies on the denseness of Lyda's character and the forcefulness of Patsy's. For instance, at the nightclub, when the MC announces there will not be a second show with Tony and Yvonne, the reporters realize something is amiss and investigate. When they see Yvonne leaving the theater, they chase her down for a scoop, leaving a card with Lyda and requesting, "Present this to the waiter when you're through." The girls finish their meal, the reporters who asked them out do not return, and Patsy admits to the waiter they have no money. The waiter tells the manager, who states that they will let it go under the circumstances of the show being cancelled. However, when he approaches the table, Patsy starts trouble right away, figuring this is a ploy to get out of paying, and the girls end up having to wash dishes. Hours later, they complete their task and Patsy indicates they are "through." Lyda says, "Oh, we are through. Then here," and presents the card the reporters gave her, which would have taken care of their meal.

A lot of elements are notable in this sequence. First, it shows the aggressive Patsy ready for an argument before realizing whether there is a conflict at all. Her confident "Leave everything to me, I'll get us out of this" is preparation for her explosive "You can't do this to me" reaction to the manager as he approaches the table, ready to let them go without paying. Secondly, there's Lyda's denseness in not presenting the card at the conclusion of the meal. Literally responding to the reporter's words "when you are through," she does not reveal she has a pass for the meal until the evening has ended. These screen personalities work for each performer and respond well enough to each other that it showed real potential for the possibility of future films together as a team.

There are also some basic elements that work here. The conflict of the narrative is established, the presence of the noted character actors Armstrong and Overman are helpful in grounding the scene, and the comedy blends nicely with the musical numbers. As Roach was trying to promote Rosina Lawrence, her chance at playing a sharp straight role is given a bit more substance and even a bit of an edge. When Yvonne slaps Tony and angrily storms out of the club and their act, she not only causes trouble for her stubborn husband, she also puts the club itself in a bind. The harried manager, the sheepish MC and the disappointed patrons are all victims of her abrupt, impulsive decision.

Meins keeps the comedy at the forefront and uses the dramatic conflict of the narrative as a backdrop. Patsy and Lyda become involved pretty quickly when they find Yvonne and her baby in the hospital. Patsy leads, and Lyda gleefully follows. However, when Patsy indicates they must sell the idea to Tony that he has become a father, the foreign-born Lyda again takes the English too literally and approaches Tony with the baby and asks if he would like to buy it. This results in a rather amusing bit of confusion. Tony is already upset at the situation his wife has left him in, and now a strange woman is trying to sell him a baby. Lyda beautifully projects pure innocence and earnestness. Tony thinks she is crazy. He even goes so far as stating it is an ugly baby!

Patsy comes into the scene to straighten everything out. But when she does so, another element of confusion arises. The reporters see her discussing the baby with Tony while holding it in her arms, and conclude that it is Patsy's baby with Tony! They set out to get a scoop out of it, even attempting to set up a wedding in the club, before realizing the truth of the situation.

One piece of the film challenges the viewer's logic. Yvonne has given birth and immediately is available to make it to the club and resume her dancing career. When illogic is found within the comedy, it is acceptable as part of the comedy. When it is found in drama, it becomes a bit sketchier. There's a lot more illogic in this movie, like the fact that Yvonne was able to hide her pregnancy for so long. (Or didn't she know she was pregnant until she gave birth? The movie isn't entirely clear on that.)

Despite the many positives, *Nobody's Baby* is limited in its aesthetic appeal. There are musical numbers that disrupt the action rather than maintaining the film's rhythmic flow, and the highlights are only mildly amusing. It is not a bad movie, however, and does serve its purpose by successfully introducing the team of Patsy Kelly and Lyda Roberti as feature film contenders.

The Motion Picture Daily reviewed *Nobody's Baby* and, while it realized the film's shortcomings, it also pointed out its highlights:

> Stretching a two-reel type of gag, dialogue and situation comedy into a feature-length farce is unexpectedly relishable when Patsy Kelly and Lyda Robert do the stretching as they have done in this film. Although much padding is introduced to gain time, the focal points are full of fun as the comediennes hop blithely in and out of the picture, a fact which creates the illusion of a speedy tempo in production. [The movie gives] Miss Kelly and Miss Roberti plenty of opportunity to be legitimately funny. Armstrong and Overman add much to the gayety of the occasion. Gus Meins' direction concentrates on getting the most from the farcical situations.[6]

Film Daily was impressed with this feature, and felt the team of Kelly and Roberti offered a lot of promise:

> This Patsy Kelly–Lyda Roberti starrer is the best thing the girls have done together and it looks like Hal Roach spent more money on this production than he did on any of their previous efforts. The piece opens with a load of slapstick comedy which moves especially fast. Then the girls become nurses and the pace slacks up. They are forced to carry the whole load and it is a little too much. Patsy's comedy antics are always good for laughs and Lyda garners her share of mussing up the English language to suit herself. Gus Meins builds a host of lightweight situations into some good laugh getters.[7]

Exhibitors indicated that their moviegoing audience members were also pleased with the proceedings, and plans were made for more Kelly–Roberti features.

Director Meins, so instrumental in the success of the Thelma Todd shorts with ZaSu Pitts and later with Patsy Kelly, was being groomed for bigger and better things, but he too left the Roach employ after this feature. The reason he gave was creative differences with the producer. Meins had no trouble securing work after leaving Roach, helming an average of five features per year in 1938 and 1939. However, after directing three films in 1940, Meins' career stalled when some extremely disturbing news about him hit the newspapers: He was accused of molesting six boys in the basement of his home.

According to the August 1, 1940, *Los Angeles Times,* "Meins, 47, awaited arraignment today on morals charges for which he vehemently claimed he could not account. In arranging a $5000 bond, Meins declared, 'For the life of me, I cannot explain or imagine how or why such charges should be brought against me. I am innocent and I will prove it.' He was arrested last night at dinner with his family." Four days later, on August 5, the *Los Angeles Times* reported that Meins had committed suicide:

> Death has halted the prosecution of morals charges against film director Gus Meins, 47, accused last Wednesday of sex offenses against six youths. Meins was found dead in his automobile, parked in brush, yesterday. Apparently he had been dead for several days. His attorney, Joseph K. Coady, expressed the belief Meins committed suicide by inhaling carbon monoxide fumes. Coady said Meins feared that publicity about his arrest would ruin his career even in the absence of any proof of guilt. Continuances were granted in the case twice when Meins failed to appear, but his $5000 bond finally was forfeited Saturday. Coady said Meins left home Wednesday night after telling his son Douglas, "You probably won't see me again." His widow was under a physician's care today.

It is an unsettling irony that Meins died in the same manner as Thelma Todd. However, while Thelma's death by inhaling carbon monoxide from a car was never solved, Meins most certainly killed himself. There are theories abounding as to Meins' guilt. Some claim that, German sentiment in America being negative during the war in Europe, Meins worried that he would not be believed. Others claim he was likely guilty and could not face the consequences. In later years, many former Our Gang members, as well as script girl Ellen Corby (the actress best known as TV's Grandma Walton, and whose husband Francis was a Roach cameraman) refused to discuss Gus Meins.

The next time that Patsy Kelly and Lyda Roberti appeared in a film together was shortly after production ended on *Nobody's Baby* in November 1936. Hal Roach wanted a vehicle to promote Rosina Lawrence so he starred her in the feature *Pick a Star,* about a small town girl entering the movie world with the help of a sharp publicity agent (Jack Haley). It was a typical story, but Roach punctuated it with appearances by Patsy, Lyda and Laurel and Hardy. Patsy does get top billing, but she does not act as part of a team. Lyda plays Dagmar, a temperamental performer. This role for Lyda has elements of the character she had played in some stage roles, and films like *Million Dollar Legs.* It is a short-tempered diva type, and Roberti plays it beautifully.

At about this time, Hal Roach studio designer Ernest Schrapps told *Film Daily* how he picked out wardrobe for the ladies[8]:

Patsy Kelly is more the sports type. Although she looks very well in formal evening wear too. Lyda Roberti wears almost any style well, but she is particularly good in evening gowns. Miss Kelly seems to be happier in dark green, dark blue, or light shades of brown. Lyda Roberti is her most charming and vivacious in a light green. Although you will see the costumes in *Pick a Star* only in black and white, you can be sure that each woman in the cast is wearing a color that she likes.

Lyda Roberti, the versatile actress who was just about to move into a possible series of feature films as part of a comedy team, had to leave the profession due to illness. Diagnosed with a heart ailment, she quit movies on doctor's orders after filming her scenes in a Joe E. Brown vehicle entitled *Wide Open Faces* (1938). With little money coming in, Lyda and her husband, radio announcer Hugh "Bud" Ernst, were struggling with expenses. In January 1938 they were sued by grocer William F. Webb for food that was delivered to her home on credit months earlier and for which he had never been paid.

On March 12, 1938, Roberti was sitting on her bed, bending over to tie her shoe, when she suffered a massive heart attack. Her husband summoned their family physician, Myron Babcock, to their apartment, and he attempted to save her life by giving her heart stimulants, but to no avail. Roberti passed away lying in her bed, with her husband at her side.

Roberti's funeral was held on March 15, 1938, with floral tributes sent by Patsy Kelly, Hal Roach, her old friend Jack Oakie from *Million Dollar Legs*, her co-star of her final movie Joe E. Brown, as well as friends like Stan Laurel, Errol Flynn, Al Jolson and Ginger Rogers. She was interred at Forest Lawn Memorial Park. Her headstone reads, "Until the day break and the shadows flee away" from the Song of Solomon. Hugh Ernst later remarried his ex-wife Betty Furness, but became despondent that he was unable to have a successful career in television as he had in radio. Ashamed that he had to rely on his successful wife's income, Ernst shot himself to death on April 11, 1950. Before doing so, he phoned a newspaper editor and told him, "Get a reporter here in ten minutes. Send him up and you'll get a story." Ernst's body was found with a newspaper clipping next to it, an article which claimed that he and Furness were on the verge of divorce. There was a piece of paper in Ernst's typewriter on which he had typed, "I am tired of everything and I'm sorry for what I'm about to do." He also sent his wife Betty Furness a note in the mail, which she received the day after his death. It read, "Sorry mommy."[9]

On May 28, 1938, reporter Jimmy Fidler stated in his column that he was standing on the street with actress Carole Lombard when Patsy Kelly drove by. Lombard said, "I wouldn't be in her shoes for a million bucks. She used to co-star in comedies with Thelma Todd and then Lyda Roberti, and they are both dead now. Death always strikes three times. I've been shuddering ever since."[10] This is especially unsettling when one recalls that Lombard would be killed in a plane crash only four years later.

Patsy Kelly told the author in 1976, "Lyda was a sweet gal and naturally funny. It was such a shame; really such a terrible shame."

8

The Later Years
of ZaSu Pitts and Patsy Kelly

When ZaSu Pitts left the Todd–Pitts comedy series, she plunged into her work as a freelancer. She left the two-reelers in 1933, and made appearances in ten feature films the following year. ZaSu lightened her activity load in the ensuing years, but made appearances in some notable films that have lived on. She and W.C. Fields were something of an afterthought when they were added to *Mrs. Wiggs of the Cabbage Patch* (1934), providing comic relief as well as some box office clout. When reporter James B. Fisher visited the set, ZaSu told him, "I don't think I'm funny. Most of the time I'm very serious." Then, pointing out Fields, she said, "There is my favorite comedian, nose and all."[1]

Her appearance in *Ruggles of Red Gap* (1935) added even more humor to an already delightful comedy. She starred as Hildegarde Withers opposite James Gleason in *The Plot Thickens* (1936) and *Forty Naughty Girls* (1937). Pitts appeared in no films released in 1938, instead opting to go on a cross-country vaudeville tour. She was hoping to land the role of ballerina Essie in the Frank Capra feature *You Can't Take It with You* (1938), which won the Oscar for Best Picture. But the role went to Ann Miller. ZaSu told the press at the time, "Essie was the perfect role for me, except that I had never danced ballet. I went to a ballet professor and said that I wanted to learn. Furthermore, I wanted to be able to whirl on my toes. I could get up on my toes all right, but the only way I could get off them was to fall flat on my face and, oh dear, I usually did. So they gave the role to Ann Miller, that Tex girl who is such a good dancer and has glamour too."[2]

ZaSu continued to appear frequently in movies right into the 1940s, including a fun role at Warner Brothers in the Humphrey Bogart feature *It All Came True*. One of her most intriguing film appearances occurred in 1941 when Hal Roach hired her to appear in his feature *Broadway Limited*, opposite none other than Patsy Kelly. Patsy and ZaSu also made some live appearances at movie houses to promote the film.

Throughout the 1930s and 1940s, Pitts also acted on stage and frequently appeared on popular radio programs. In 1942, she toured the Midwest in a stage show entitled *Her First Murder*. She made her Broadway debut in 1943 with a play written especially for her, *Ramshackle Inn*. Prior to its Broadway opening, the play was performed as a tryout in Norfolk, Virginia. In an interview at the time, ZaSu recalled sharing a train with young soldiers:

> The train was so crowded we took turns sitting down, and it wasn't possible to walk in the aisle without warning the standees to hold their breath. We shared seats and fruit and books. All those fine young lads had stayed with their families until the last possible minute of their furloughs. They had to get back to camp. We in the cast were just en route to put on a show.[3]

That same playwright, George Batson, wrote another play for Pitts, *Cordelia*, in which she appeared on tour in 1946.

In the 1950s, Pitts did television work, including a version of the George Kaufman–Moss Hart play *The Man Who Came to Dinner*, playing Miss Preen to Monty Woolley's Sheridan Whiteside. The cast also boasted Buster Keaton, Margaret Hamilton, Bert Lahr and Reginald Gardiner. Pitts co-starred on *The Gale Storm Show* (aka *Oh Susanna*), which ran a respectable four seasons (1956–1960). This part won ZaSu a new generation of fans who were not old enough to have seen her two-reelers with Thelma Todd. The series was shot at the Hal Roach Studios, now run by Hal Roach, Jr. ZaSu told the press, "Gale Storm is as dear to me as my own daughter. And Hal Roach, Sr., still drops by on the set for a chat about the old days. He likes to tease me, saying I have not aged a bit. They all take care of me."[4]

Throughout the '50s and '60s, ZaSu continued to do TV guest shots on shows such as *Guestward Ho, Perry Mason* and *Burke's Law*. She also showed up in the occasional film, including *Teenage Millionaire* (1961) and *The Thrill of It All* (1963).

Pitts was diagnosed with cancer as far back as 1956, but recovered well enough to continue working. She finally succumbed to cancer on June 7, 1963, at age 69. Her last film appearance was in Stanley Kramer's all-star comedy epic *It's a Mad Mad Mad Mad World*, which was released posthumously.

Patsy Kelly, a sought-after character actress, had no trouble securing work in movies. In 1938, she was cast in the Hal Roach–produced feature *Merrily We Live*, which was nominated for five Oscars. She followed that up with *The Cowboy and the Lady*, which starred Gary Cooper, and then went into *The Gorilla* starring the zany Ritz Brothers and featuring Bela Lugosi. By the early 1940s, her popularity in movies started to wane. Unlike a lot of gay Hollywood stars during this period, Patsy was not closeted. In interviews she would proudly proclaim herself to be "a dyke" and claimed to be in a relationship with actress Wilma Cox, a Roach actress who appeared in films with Charley Chase and Our Gang (and with Patsy in *Pick a Star, Nobody's Baby* and *Merrily We Live*).

By 1943, Kelly was no longer securing good roles in movies, so she left the motion picture industry, remaining off-screen for 17 years, and moved to New York, where she worked on stage and in radio. Patsy also worked as Tallulah Bankhead's secretary and companion, claiming they also had a sexual relationship during their time together.

In the 1950s, Patsy slowly got back into screen acting via television and in 1960 began taking on occasional movie roles with her appearance in the family film *Please Don't Eat the Daisies*. Patsy did more work in television than theatrical films during the 1960s with appearances on such shows as *The Untouchables, The Man from U.N.C.L.E.* and *Bonanza*. She often wasted her time and talent in throwaway movies like *The Ghost in the Invisible Bikini* and *C'mon Let's Live a Little*, but she scored with her performance in Roman Polanski's *Rosemary's Baby* (1968).

In the 1970s, Kelly returned to where she started, the Broadway stage. She earned a Tony for her performance in the hit revival of the musical *No No Nanette* in 1971. She was nominated again the following year for *Irene*, which featured Debbie Reynolds.

The '70s was the final decade that Patsy Kelly was active in show business. In January 1980, after making appearances in the Disney movies *Freaky Friday* and *North Avenue Irregulars* and a role on TV's *The Love Boat*, she suffered a massive stroke that left her unable to speak. She died on September 24, 1981.

Chapter Notes

Chapter 1

1. "Let's Do Things," *Motion Picture World*, September 5, 1931.
2. "Let's Do Things," *New Movie Magazine*, February, 1932.
3. Bartee Haile, "Big Boy Williams Has Eerie Premonition of His Death," *San Marcos Mercury*, August 23, 2012.
4. "Catch-As Catch-Can," *Film Daily*, February 14, 1932.
5. "Pajama Party," *Variety*, November 3, 1931.
6. "Pajama Party," *Film Daily*, October 18, 1931.
7. "War Mamas," *Film Daily*, December 27, 1931.
8. "War Mamas," *Motion Picture Herald*, May 7, 1932.
9. Morgan Michelle, *The Ice Cream Blonde: The Whirlwind Life and Mysterious Death of Screwball Comedienne Thelma Todd,* (Chicago: Chicago Review Press, 2015).
10. Thomas, Dan, "How Thelma Became a New Woman," *Arizona Daily Star*, September 27, 1931.
11. It is obvious that Laurel and Hardy shot their scene separately when they had a break on one of their own films, and their fleeing of flying objects was edited together with Thelma and ZaSu throwing them, but the scene still works.
12. "The Old Bull," *Motion Picture Herald*, May 7, 1932.
13. "The Old Bull," *Film Daily*, May 5, 1932.
14. "The Old Bull," *Variety* October, 4,1932.
15. "More Todd-Pitts Shorts," *Variety*, March 22, 1932.
16. "Show Business," *Variety*, November 6, 1932.
17. "Show Business," *Film Daily*, October 11, 1932.
18. "Show Business," *Motion Picture Herald*, May 20, 1933.
19. "Alum and Eve," *Motion Picture Herald*, August 13, 1932.
20. "Alum and Eve," *Film Daily*, February 16, 1933.
21. "A Little from the Lots," *Film Daily*, September 12, 1932.
22. Michelle, *The Ice Cream Blonde*.
23. "Zasu Pitts and Thelma Todd Click Again," *Hollywood Filmograph*, December 31, 1932.
24. George "Spanky" McFarland, interview with the author, 1980.
25. Michelle, *The Ice Cream Blonde*.
26. Hal Roach Cuts Shorts Program To 40 Subjects, *Hollywood Reporter*, May 19, 1933.
27. Hal Roach Studio Stars Work Again, *Hollywood Reporter*, June 3, 1933.

Chapter 2

1. "Have You Seen Kelly," by Dena Reed, *Screenland* April, 1935.
2. Interview with the author, 1976.
3. Ralph Wilk, "A Little from Lots," *Film Daily*, October 6, 1933.
4. "Babes in the Goods," *Film Daily*, March 1, 1934.
5. "Babes in the Goods," *Motion Picture Daily*, March 5, 1934.
6. "I'll Be Suing You," *Variety*, November 20, 1934.
7. "Three Chumps Ahead," *Variety*, October 30, 1934.
8. "Done in Oil," *Motion Picture Herald*, November 10, 1934.
9. "Done in Oil," *Motion Picture Daily*, November 16, 1934.
10. "Done in Oil," *Film Daily*, November 3, 1934.

11. Morgan Michelle, *The Ice Cream Blonde: The Whirlwind Life and Mysterious Death of Screwball Comedienne Thelma Todd* (Chicago: Chicago Review Press, 2015).
12. "Bum Voyage," *Variety*, May 15, 1935.
13. "Bum Voyage," *Film Daily*, April 12, 1935.
14. Dena Reed, "Have You Seen Kelly," *Screenland*, April, 1935.
15. "Treasure Blues," *Film Daily*, June 4, 1935.
16. "Sing Sister Sing," *Film Daily*, July 26, 1935.
17. Julia Gwin, "It Comes Out Here," *Screenland*, March, 1936.
18. "The Tin Man," *Film Daily*, March 23, 1935.
19. "The Misses Stooge," *Film Daily*, June 12, 1935.
20. Peter B. Flint, "Patsy Kelly, Actress Is Dead: Played Comic Roles in Films," *New York Times*, September 26, 1981.
21. Michelle, *The Ice Cream Blonde*.

Chapter 3

1. Ramona Bergere, "She Does as She Pleases," *Modern Screen*, March, 1937.
2. Jack Smalley, "Tragedy Taught Lyda Roberti to Smile," *Movie Classic*, April, 1935.

3. "In Hollywood," (syndicated), *Edwardsville Intelligencer*, September 17, 1936.
4. "Hill Tillies," *Film Daily* June 9, 1936.
5. George McFarland interview with the author, 1980.
6. "Nobody's Baby," *Motion Picture Daily*, January 29, 1937.
7. "Nobody's Baby," *Film Daily*, February 2, 1937.
8. "And Now Enter the Fashionable Comediennes," *Film Daily*, March 15, 1937.
9. "Hugh 'Bud' Ernst—Best Friend to Errol Flynn," *The Errol Flynn Blog*, http://www.theerrolflynnblog.com/2010/07/02/hugh-bud-ernst-best-friend-to-errol-flynn/.
10. Jimmy Fidler, "In Hollywood," *Long Island Daily Press* (syndicated), May 28, 1938.

Chapter 8

1. James B. Fisher, "I Don't Think I'm Funny," *Screenland*, October, 1934.
2. Charles Stumpf, *ZaSu Pitts: The Life and Career* (Jefferson, NC: McFarland, 2010).
3. Stumpf, *ZaSu Pitts*.
4. Stumpf, *ZaSu Pitts*.

Bibliography

Books

Anthony, Brian, and Andy Edmonds. *Smile When the Raindrops Fall*. Lanham, MD: Scarecrow Press, 1998.

Calman, Craig. *100 Years of Brodies with Hal Roach: The Jaunty Journeys of a Hollywood Motion Picture and Television Pioneer*. Albany, GA: Bear Manor Media, 2014.

Edmonds, Andy. *Hot Toddy: The True Story of Hollywood's Most Shocking Crime: The Murder of Thelma Todd*. New York: William Morrow, 1989.

Bowles, Stephen E. *The Film Anthologies Index*. Metuchen, NJ: Scarecrow Press, 1994.

Donati, William. *The Life and Death of Thelma Todd*. Jefferson, NC: McFarland, 2012.

Doyle, Billy H. *The Ultimate Directory of Silent and Sound Era Performers*. Metuchen, NJ: Scarecrow Press, 1999.

Edmonds, Andi. *Hot Toddy: The True Story of Hollywood's Most Shocking Crime: The Murder of Thelma Todd*. New York: Avon Books, 1991.

Everson, William K. *The Films of Hal Roach* New York: Museum of Modern Art, 1972.

Maltin, Leonard. *The Great Movie Shorts* New York: Crown Publishers, 1972.

Maltin, Leonard. *Movie Comedy Teams*. New York: Signet, 1974.

Maltin, Leonard. *The Great Movie Comedians* New York: Crown Publishers, 1978.

Maltin, Leonard, and Richard W. Bann. *Our Gang: The Life and Times of the Little Rascals*. New York: Crown Publishers, 1984.

Morgan, Michelle. *The Ice Cream Blonde: The Whirlwind Life and Mysterious Death of Screwball Comedienne Thelma Todd*. Chicago: Chicago Review Press, 2015.

Neibaur, James L. *Movie Comedians*. Jefferson, NC: McFarland, 1986.

Neibaur, James L. *The Charley Chase Talkies*. Lanham, MD: Scarecrow Press, 2013.

Skretvedt, Randy. *Laurel and Hardy: The Magic Behind the Movies*. Irvine, CA: Bonaventure Press, 2016.

Stumpf, Charles. *ZaSu Pitts: The Life and Career*. Jefferson, NC: McFarland, 2010.

Articles

"And Now Enter the Fashionable Comediennes." *Film Daily*, March 15, 1937.

Bergere, Ramona. "She Does as She Pleases." *Modern Screen* March, 1937.

Carroll, Llewellyn. "What Hollywood Did to a New England Schoolmarm." *Photoplay*, February 1932.

Fidler, Jimmy. "In Hollywood" (syndicated). *Long Island Daily Press*, May 28, 1938.

Flint, Peter B. "Patsy Kelly, Actress is Dead: Played Comic Roles in Films." *The New York Times*, September 26, 1981.

Gwin, Julia. "It Comes Out Here." *Screenland*, March 1936.

Haile, Bartee. "Big Boy Williams Has Eerie Premonition of His Death." *San Marcos Mercury*, August 23, 2012.

"Hal Roach Cuts Shorts Program To 40 Subjects." *Hollywood Reporter*, May 19, 1933.

"Hal Roach Studio Stars Work Again." *Hollywood Reporter*, June 3, 1933.

"Hollywood Producer Faces Morals Charge." *The Los Angeles Times*, August 1, 1940.

"In Hollywood" (syndicated). *Edwardsville Intelligencer*, September 17, 1936.

"Movie Director Named in Morals Case Suicide." *The Los Angeles Times*, August 5, 1940.

Reed, Dena. "Have You Seen Kelly" *Screen-land*, April 1935.

"Roach Signs Roberti." *Film Daily,* May 5, 1936.

Smalley, Jack. "Tragedy Taught Lyda Roberti to Smile." *Movie Classic*, April 1935.

Thomas, Dan. "How Thelma Became a New Woman." *Arizona Daily Star*, September 27, 1931.

Variety Staff. "More Todd-Pitts Shorts" *Variety*, March 22, 1932.

Wilk, Ralph "A Little From Lots." *Film Daily,* September 12, 1932.

Wilk, Ralph. "A Little From Lots." *Film Daily,* October 6, 1933.

"Zasu Pitts and Thelma Todd Click Again." *Hollywood Filmograph*, December 31, 1932.

Reviews

"Alum and Eve." *Motion Picture Herald*, August 13, 1932.

"Alum and Eve." *Film Daily*, February 16, 1933.

"Babes in the Goods." *Film Daily,* March 1, 1934.

"Babes in the Goods." *Motion Picture Daily,* March 5, 1934.

"Bum Voyage." *Film Daily,* April 12, 1935.

"Bum Voyage." *Variety*, May 15, 1935.

"Catch-As Catch-Can." *Film Daily*, February 14, 1932.

"Hill Tillies." *Film Daily*, June 9, 1936.

"I'll Be Suing You." *Variety*, November 20, 1934.

"The Misses Stooge." *Film Daily,* June 12, 1935.

"Nobody's Baby." *Motion Picture Daily*, January 29, 1937.

"Nobody's Baby." *Film Daily,* February 2, 1937.

"The Old Bull." *Motion Picture Herald*, May 7, 1932.

"The Old Bull." *Film Daily*, May 5, 1932.

"The Old Bull." *Variety*, October 4,1932.

"Pajama Party." *Variety*, November 3, 1931.

"Pajama Party." *Film Daily*, October 18, 1931.

"Show Business." *Variety*, November 6, 1932.

"Show Business." *Film Daily*, October 11, 1932.

"Show Business." *Motion Picture Herald*, May 20, 1933.

"Sing Sister Sing." *Film Daily,* July 26, 1935.

"Three Chumps Ahead." *Variety,* October 30, 1934.

"The Tin Man." *Film Daily*, March 23, 1935.

"War Mamas." *Film Daily*, December 27, 1931.

"War Mamas." *Motion Picture Herald*, May 7, 1932.

Interviews

Patsy Kelly, with the author, 1976.

George McFarland, with the author, 1980.

Online

Another Fine Mess: The Films of the Hal Roach Studios

Facebook: The Hal Roach Studio group

Facebook: The Thelma Todd Fan Group

"Hugh 'Bud' Ernst—Best Friend to Errol Flynn." The Errol Flynn Blog

The Internet Broadway Database

The Internet Movie Database

Nitrateville

TV.Com

Twitter

Wikipedia

Index

Index